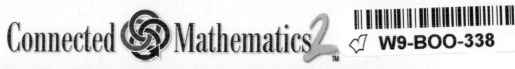

Connected Mathematics 2™

Comparing and Scaling

Ratio, Proportion, and Percent

Glenda Lappan

James T. Fey

William M. Fitzgerald

Susan N. Friel

Elizabeth Difanis Phillips

PEARSON

Prentice Hall

Boston, Massachusetts
Upper Saddle River, New Jersey

Connected Mathematics™ was developed at Michigan State University with financial support from the Michigan State University Office of the Provost, Computing and Technology, and the College of Natural Science.

This material is based upon work supported by the National Science Foundation under Grant No. MDR 9150217 and Grant No. ESI 9986372. Opinions expressed are those of the authors and not necessarily those of the Foundation.

The Michigan State University authors and administration have agreed that all MSU royalties arising from this publication will be devoted to purposes supported by the MSU Mathematics Education Enrichment Fund.

Acknowledgments appear on page 72, which constitutes an extension of this copyright page.

Authors of Connected Mathematics

(from left to right) Glenda Lappan, Betty Phillips, Susan Friel, Bill Fitzgerald, Jim Fey

Glenda Lappan is a University Distinguished Professor in the Department of Mathematics at Michigan State University. Her research and development interests are in the connected areas of students' learning of mathematics and mathematics teachers' professional growth and change related to the development and enactment of K–12 curriculum materials.

James T. Fey is a Professor of Curriculum and Instruction and Mathematics at the University of Maryland. His consistent professional interest has been development and research focused on curriculum materials that engage middle and high school students in problem-based collaborative investigations of mathematical ideas and their applications.

William M. Fitzgerald (*Deceased*) was a Professor in the Department of Mathematics at Michigan State University. His early research was on the use of concrete materials in supporting student learning and led to the development of teaching materials for laboratory environments. Later he helped develop a teaching model to support student experimentation with mathematics.

Susan N. Friel is a Professor of Mathematics Education in the School of Education at the University of North Carolina at Chapel Hill. Her research interests focus on statistics education for middle-grade students and, more broadly, on teachers' professional development and growth in teaching mathematics K–8.

Elizabeth Difanis Phillips is a Senior Academic Specialist in the Mathematics Department of Michigan State University. She is interested in teaching and learning mathematics for both teachers and students. These interests have led to curriculum and professional development projects at the middle school and high school levels, as well as projects related to the teaching and learning of algebra across the grades.

CMP2 Development Staff

Teacher Collaborator in Residence
Yvonne Grant
Michigan State University

Administrative Assistant
Judith Martus Miller
Michigan State University

Production and Field Site Manager
Lisa Keller
Michigan State University

Technical and Editorial Support
Brin Keller, Peter Lappan, Jim Laser,
Michael Masterson, Stacey Miceli

Assessment Team
June Bailey and Debra Sobko (Apollo Middle School, Rochester, New York), George Bright (University of North Carolina, Greensboro), Gwen Ranzau Campbell (Sunrise Park Middle School, White Bear Lake, Minnesota), Holly DeRosia, Kathy Dole, and Teri Keusch (Portland Middle School, Portland, Michigan), Mary Beth Schmitt (Traverse City East Junior High School, Traverse City, Michigan), Genni Steele (Central Middle School, White Bear Lake, Minnesota), Jacqueline Stewart (Okemos, Michigan), Elizabeth Tye (Magnolia Junior High School, Magnolia, Arkansas)

Development Assistants
At Lansing Community College *Undergraduate Assistant:* James Brinegar

At Michigan State University *Graduate Assistants:* Dawn Berk, Emily Bouck, Bulent Buyukbozkirli, Kuo-Liang Chang, Christopher Danielson, Srinivasa Dharmavaram, Deb Johanning, Kelly Rivette, Sarah Sword, Tat Ming Sze, Marie Turini, Jeffrey Wanko; *Undergraduate Assistants:* Jeffrey Chapin, Jade Corsé, Elisha Hardy, Alisha Harold, Elizabeth Keusch, Julia Letoutchaia, Karen Loeffler, Brian Oliver, Carl Oliver, Evonne Pedawi, Lauren Rebrovich

At the University of Maryland *Graduate Assistants:* Kim Harris Bethea, Kara Karch

At the University of North Carolina (Chapel Hill) *Graduate Assistants:* Mark Ellis, Trista Stearns; *Undergraduate Assistant:* Daniel Smith

Advisory Board for CMP2

Thomas Banchoff
Professor of Mathematics
Brown University
Providence, Rhode Island

Anne Bartel
Mathematics Coordinator
Minneapolis Public Schools
Minneapolis, Minnesota

Hyman Bass
Professor of Mathematics
University of Michigan
Ann Arbor, Michigan

Joan Ferrini-Mundy
Associate Dean of the College of
Natural Science; Professor
Michigan State University
East Lansing, Michigan

James Hiebert
Professor
University of Delaware
Newark, Delaware

Susan Hudson Hull
Charles A. Dana Center
University of Texas
Austin, Texas

Michele Luke
Mathematics Curriculum
Coordinator
West Junior High
Minnetonka, Minnesota

Kay McClain
Assistant Professor of
Mathematics Education
Vanderbilt University
Nashville, Tennessee

Edward Silver
Professor; Chair of Educational
Studies
University of Michigan
Ann Arbor, Michigan

Judith Sowder
Professor Emerita
San Diego State University
San Diego, California

Lisa Usher
Mathematics Resource Teacher
California Academy of
Mathematics and Science
San Pedro, California

Field Test Sites for CMP2

During the development of the revised edition of *Connected Mathematics* (CMP2), more than 100 classroom teachers have field-tested materials at 49 school sites in 12 states and the District of Columbia. This classroom testing occurred over three academic years (2001 through 2004), allowing careful study of the effectiveness of each of the 24 units that comprise the program. A special thanks to the students and teachers at these pilot schools.

Arkansas

Magnolia Public Schools
Kittena Bell*, Judith Trowell*; *Central Elementary School:* Maxine Broom, Betty Eddy, Tiffany Fallin, Bonnie Flurry, Carolyn Monk, Elizabeth Tye; *Magnolia Junior High School:* Monique Bryan, Ginger Cook, David Graham, Shelby Lamkin

Colorado

Boulder Public Schools
Nevin Platt Middle School: Judith Koenig

St. Vrain Valley School District, Longmont
Westview Middle School: Colleen Beyer, Kitty Canupp, Ellie Decker*, Peggy McCarthy, Tanya deNobrega, Cindy Payne, Ericka Pilon, Andrew Roberts

District of Columbia

Capitol Hill Day School: Ann Lawrence

Georgia

University of Georgia, Athens
Brad Findell

Madison Public Schools
Morgan County Middle School: Renee Burgdorf, Lynn Harris, Nancy Kurtz, Carolyn Stewart

Maine

Falmouth Public Schools
Falmouth Middle School: Donna Erikson, Joyce Hebert, Paula Hodgkins, Rick Hogan, David Legere, Cynthia Martin, Barbara Stiles, Shawn Towle*

* indicates a Field Test Site Coordinator

Michigan

Portland Public Schools
Portland Middle School: Mark Braun, Holly DeRosia, Kathy Dole*, Angie Foote, Teri Keusch, Tammi Wardwell

Traverse City Area Public Schools
Bertha Vos Elementary: Kristin Sak; *Central Grade School:* Michelle Clark; Jody Meyers; *Eastern Elementary:* Karrie Tufts; *Interlochen Elementary:* Mary McGee-Cullen; *Long Lake Elementary:* Julie Faulkner*, Charlie Maxbauer, Katherine Sleder; *Norris Elementary:* Hope Slanaker; *Oak Park Elementary:* Jessica Steed; *Traverse Heights Elementary:* Jennifer Wolfert; *Westwoods Elementary:* Nancy Conn; *Old Mission Peninsula School:* Deb Larimer; *Traverse City East Junior High:* Ivanka Berkshire, Ruthanne Kladder, Jan Palkowski, Jane Peterson, Mary Beth Schmitt; *Traverse City West Junior High:* Dan Fouch*, Ray Fouch

Sturgis Public Schools
Sturgis Middle School: Ellen Eisele

Minnesota

Burnsville School District 191
Hidden Valley Elementary: Stephanie Cin, Jane McDevitt

Hopkins School District 270
Alice Smith Elementary: Sandra Cowing, Kathleen Gustafson, Martha Mason, Scott Stillman; *Eisenhower Elementary:* Chad Bellig, Patrick Berger, Nancy Glades, Kye Johnson, Shane Wasserman, Victoria Wilson; *Gatewood Elementary:* Sarah Ham, Julie Kloos, Janine Pung, Larry Wade; *Glen Lake Elementary:* Jacqueline Cramer, Kathy Hering, Cecelia Morris,

Robb Trenda; *Katherine Curren Elementary:* Diane Bancroft, Sue DeWit, John Wilson; *L. H. Tanglen Elementary:* Kevin Athmann, Lisa Becker, Mary LaBelle, Kathy Rezac, Roberta Severson; *Meadowbrook Elementary:* Jan Gauger, Hildy Shank, Jessica Zimmerman; *North Junior High:* Laurel Hahn, Kristin Lee, Jodi Markuson, Bruce Mestemacher, Laurel Miller, Bonnie Rinker, Jeannine Salzer, Sarah Shafer, Cam Stottler; *West Junior High:* Alicia Beebe, Kristie Earl, Nobu Fujii, Pam Georgetti, Susan Gilbert, Regina Nelson Johnson, Debra Lindstrom, Michele Luke*, Jon Sorenson

Minneapolis School District 1
Ann Sullivan K-8 School: Bronwyn Collins; Anne Bartel* (Curriculum and Instruction Office)

Wayzata School District 284
Central Middle School: Sarajane Myers, Dan Nielsen, Tanya Ravenholdt

White Bear Lake School District 624
Central Middle School: Amy Jorgenson, Michelle Reich, Brenda Sammon

New York

New York City Public Schools
IS 89: Yelena Aynbinder, Chi-Man Ng, Nina Rapaport, Joel Spengler, Phyllis Tam*, Brent Wyso; *Wagner Middle School:* Jason Appel, Intissar Fernandez, Yee Gee Get, Richard Goldstein, Irving Marcus, Sue Norton, Bernadita Owens, Jennifer Rehn*, Kevin Yuhas

Ohio

Talawanda School District, Oxford
Talawanda Middle School: Teresa Abrams, Larry Brock, Heather Brosey, Julie Churchman, Monna Even, Karen Fitch, Bob George, Amanda Klee, Pat Meade, Sandy Montgomery, Barbara Sherman, Lauren Steidl

Miami University
Jeffrey Wanko*

Springfield Public Schools
Rockway School: Jim Mamer

Pennsylvania

Pittsburgh Public Schools
Kenneth Labuskes, Marianne O'Connor, Mary Lynn Raith*; *Arthur J. Rooney Middle School:* David Hairston, Stamatina Mousetis, Alfredo Zangaro; *Frick International Studies Academy:* Suzanne Berry, Janet Falkowski, Constance Finseth, Romika Hodge, Frank Machi; *Reizenstein Middle School:* Jeff Baldwin, James Brautigam, Lorena Burnett, Glen Cobbett, Michael Jordan, Margaret Lazur, Melissa Munnell, Holly Neely, Ingrid Reed, Dennis Reft

Texas

Austin Independent School District
Bedichek Middle School: Lisa Brown, Jennifer Glasscock, Vicki Massey

El Paso Independent School District
Cordova Middle School: Armando Aguirre, Anneliesa Durkes, Sylvia Guzman, Pat Holguin*, William Holguin, Nancy Nava, Laura Orozco, Michelle Peña, Roberta Rosen, Patsy Smith, Jeremy Wolf

Plano Independent School District
Patt Henry, James Wohlgehagen*; *Frankford Middle School:* Mandy Baker, Cheryl Butsch, Amy Dudley, Betsy Eshelman, Janet Greene, Cort Haynes, Kathy Letchworth, Kay Marshall, Kelly McCants, Amy Reck, Judy Scott, Syndy Snyder, Lisa Wang; *Wilson Middle School:* Darcie Bane, Amanda Bedenko, Whitney Evans, Tonelli Hatley, Sarah (Becky) Higgs, Kelly Johnston, Rebecca McElligott, Kay Neuse, Cheri Slocum, Kelli Straight

Washington

Evergreen School District
Shahala Middle School: Nicole Abrahamsen, Terry Coon*, Carey Doyle, Sheryl Drechsler, George Gemma, Gina Helland, Amy Hilario, Darla Lidyard, Sean McCarthy, Tilly Meyer, Willow Neuwelt, Todd Parsons, Brian Pederson, Stan Posey, Shawn Scott, Craig Sjoberg, Lynette Sundstrom, Charles Switzer, Luke Youngblood

Wisconsin

Beaver Dam Unified School District
Beaver Dam Middle School: Jim Braemer, Jeanne Frick, Jessica Greatens, Barbara Link, Dennis McCormick, Karen Michels, Nancy Nichols*, Nancy Palm, Shelly Stelsel, Susan Wiggins

Milwaukee Public Schools
Fritsche Middle School: Peggy Brokaw, Rosann Hollinger*, Dan Homontowski, David Larson, LaRon Ramsey, Judy Roschke*, Lora Ruedt, Dorothy Schuller, Sandra Wiesen, Aaron Womack, Jr.

---

* indicates a Field Test Site Coordinator

Reviews of CMP to Guide Development of CMP2

Before writing for CMP2 began or field tests were conducted, the first edition of *Connected Mathematics* was submitted to the mathematics faculties of school districts from many parts of the country and to 80 individual reviewers for extensive comments.

School District Survey Reviews of CMP

Arizona
Madison School District #38 (Phoenix)

Arkansas
Cabot School District, Little Rock School District, Magnolia School District

California
Los Angeles Unified School District

Colorado
St. Vrain Valley School District (Longmont)

Florida
Leon County Schools (Tallahassee)

Illinois
School District #21 (Wheeling)

Indiana
Joseph L. Block Junior High (East Chicago)

Kentucky
Fayette County Public Schools (Lexington)

Maine
Selection of Schools

Massachusetts
Selection of Schools

Michigan
Sparta Area Schools

Minnesota
Hopkins School District

Texas
Austin Independent School District, The El Paso Collaborative for Academic Excellence, Plano Independent School District

Wisconsin
Platteville Middle School

Individual Reviewers of CMP

Arkansas
Deborah Cramer; Robby Frizzell *(Taylor)*; Lowell Lynde *(University of Arkansas, Monticello)*; Leigh Manzer *(Norfork)*; Lynne Roberts *(Emerson High School, Emerson)*; Tony Timms *(Cabot Public Schools)*; Judith Trowell *(Arkansas Department of Higher Education)*

California
José Alcantar *(Gilroy)*; Eugenie Belcher *(Gilroy)*; Marian Pasternack *(Lowman M. S. T. Center, North Hollywood)*; Susana Pezoa *(San Jose)*; Todd Rabusin *(Hollister)*; Margaret Siegfried *(Ocala Middle School, San Jose)*; Polly Underwood *(Ocala Middle School, San Jose)*

Colorado
Janeane Golliher *(St. Vrain Valley School District, Longmont)*; Judith Koenig *(Nevin Platt Middle School, Boulder)*

Florida
Paige Loggins *(Swift Creek Middle School, Tallahassee)*

Illinois
Jan Robinson *(School District #21, Wheeling)*

Indiana
Frances Jackson *(Joseph L. Block Junior High, East Chicago)*

Kentucky
Natalee Feese *(Fayette County Public Schools, Lexington)*

Maine
Betsy Berry *(Maine Math & Science Alliance, Augusta)*

Maryland
Joseph Gagnon *(University of Maryland, College Park)*; Paula Maccini *(University of Maryland, College Park)*

Massachusetts
George Cobb *(Mt. Holyoke College, South Hadley)*; Cliff Kanold *(University of Massachusetts, Amherst)*

Michigan
Mary Bouck *(Farwell Area Schools)*; Carol Dorer *(Slauson Middle School, Ann Arbor)*; Carrie Heancy *(Forsythe Middle School, Ann Arbor)*; Ellen Hopkins *(Clague Middle School, Ann Arbor)*; Teri Keusch *(Portland Middle School, Portland)*; Valerie Mills *(Oakland Schools, Waterford)*; Mary Beth Schmitt *(Traverse City East Junior High, Traverse City)*; Jack Smith *(Michigan State University, East Lansing)*; Rebecca Spencer *(Sparta Middle School, Sparta)*; Ann Marie Nicoll Turner *(Tappan Middle School, Ann Arbor)*; Scott Turner *(Scarlett Middle School, Ann Arbor)*

Minnesota
Margarita Alvarez *(Olson Middle School, Minneapolis)*; Jane Amundson *(Nicollet Junior High, Burnsville)*; Anne Bartel *(Minneapolis Public Schools)*; Gwen Ranzau Campbell *(Sunrise Park Middle School, White Bear Lake)*; Stephanie Cin *(Hidden Valley Elementary, Burnsville)*; Joan Garfield *(University of Minnesota, Minneapolis)*; Gretchen Hall *(Richfield Middle School, Richfield)*; Jennifer Larson *(Olson Middle School, Minneapolis)*; Michele Luke *(West Junior High, Minnetonka)*; Jeni Meyer *(Richfield Junior High, Richfield)*; Judy Pfingsten *(Inver Grove Heights Middle School, Inver Grove Heights)*; Sarah Shafer *(North Junior High, Minnetonka)*; Genni Steele *(Central Middle School, White Bear Lake)*; Victoria Wilson *(Eisenhower Elementary, Hopkins)*; Paul Zorn *(St. Olaf College, Northfield)*

New York
Debra Altenau-Bartolino *(Greenwich Village Middle School, New York)*; Doug Clements *(University of Buffalo)*; Francis Curcio *(New York University, New York)*; Christine Dorosh *(Clinton School for Writers, Brooklyn)*; Jennifer Rehn *(East Side Middle School, New York)*; Phyllis Tam *(IS 89 Lab School, New York)*;

Marie Turini *(Louis Armstrong Middle School, New York)*; Lucy West *(Community School District 2, New York)*; Monica Witt *(Simon Baruch Intermediate School 104, New York)*

Pennsylvania
Robert Aglietti *(Pittsburgh)*; Sharon Mihalich *(Pittsburgh)*; Jennifer Plumb *(South Hills Middle School, Pittsburgh)*; Mary Lynn Raith *(Pittsburgh Public Schools)*

Texas
Michelle Bittick *(Austin Independent School District)*; Margaret Cregg *(Plano Independent School District)*; Sheila Cunningham *(Klein Independent School District)*; Judy Hill *(Austin Independent School District)*; Patricia Holguin *(El Paso Independent School District)*; Bonnie McNemar *(Arlington)*; Kay Neuse *(Plano Independent School District)*; Joyce Polanco *(Austin Independent School District)*; Marge Ramirez *(University of Texas at El Paso)*; Pat Rossman *(Baker Campus, Austin)*; Cindy Schimek *(Houston)*; Cynthia Schneider *(Charles A. Dana Center, University of Texas at Austin)*; Uri Treisman *(Charles A. Dana Center, University of Texas at Austin)*; Jacqueline Weilmuenster *(Grapevine-Colleyville Independent School District)*; LuAnn Weynand *(San Antonio)*; Carmen Whitman *(Austin Independent School District)*; James Wohlgehagen *(Plano Independent School District)*

Washington
Ramesh Gangolli *(University of Washington, Seattle)*

Wisconsin
Susan Lamon *(Marquette University, Hales Corner)*; Steve Reinhart *(retired, Chippewa Falls Middle School, Eau Claire)*

Table of Contents

Comparing and Scaling
Ratio, Proportion, and Percent

Comparing and Scaling

Ratio, Proportion, and Percent

At camp, Miriam uses a pottery wheel to make 3 bowls in 2 hours. Duane makes 5 bowls in 3 hours. Who is the faster potter? Suppose they continue to work at the same pace. How long will it take each of them to make a set of 12 bowls?

It takes 100 maple trees to make 25 gallons of maple syrup. How many maple trees does it take for one gallon of syrup?

Two summers ago, a biologist captured, tagged, and released 20 puffins on an island. When she returned this past summer, she captured 50 puffins. Two of them were tagged. About how many puffins are on the island?

Many everyday problems and decisions call for comparisons. Which car is safer? Which horse is the fastest? Which Internet service is cheaper? In some cases, the comparisons involve only counting, measuring, or rating, then ordering the results from least to greatest. In other cases, more complex reasoning is required.

How would you answer the comparison questions on the previous page?

In this unit, you will explore many ways to compare numbers. You'll learn how to both choose and use the best comparison strategies to solve problems and make decisions.

Mathematical Highlights

Ratio, Proportion, and Percent

In *Comparing and Scaling*, you will develop several methods for comparing quantities. You will use these methods to solve problems.

___

You will learn how to

- Use informal language to ask comparison questions

    Examples:

    "What is the ratio of boys to girls in our class?"

    "What fraction of the class is going to the spring picnic?"

    "What percent of the girls play basketball?"

    "Which model of car has the best fuel economy?"

- Choose an appropriate method to make comparisons among quantities using ratios, percents, fractions, rates, or differences

- Find equivalent forms of given ratios and rates to scale comparisons up and down

- Find and interpret unit rates, and use them to make comparisons

- Use unit rates to write an equation to represent a pattern in a table of data

- Set up and solve proportions

- Use proportional reasoning to solve problems

As you work on the problems in this unit, ask yourself questions about problem situations that involve comparisons:

What quantities should be compared?

What type of comparison will give the most useful information?

How can the comparison be expressed in different but useful ways?

How can given comparison data be used to make predictions about unknown quantities?

Making Comparisons

Surveys may report people's preferences in food, cars, or political candidates. Often, the favorites are easy to recognize. Explaining how much more popular one choice is than another can be more difficult. In this investigation, you will explore strategies for comparing numbers in accurate and useful ways. As you work on the problems, notice how the different ways of making comparisons send different messages about the numbers being compared.

1.1 Ads That Sell

An ad for the soft drink Bolda Cola starts like this:

To complete the ad, the Bolda Cola company plans to report the results of taste tests. A copywriter for the ad department has proposed four possible conclusions.

1. In a taste test, people who preferred Bolda Cola outnumbered those who preferred Cola Nola by a ratio of 17,139 to 11,426.

2. In a taste test, 5,713 more people preferred Bolda Cola.

3. In a taste test, 60% of the people preferred Bolda Cola.

4. In a taste test, people who preferred Bolda Cola outnumbered those who preferred Cola Nola by a ratio of 3 to 2.

Problem 1.1 Exploring Ratios and Rates

A. Describe what you think each statement above means.

B. Which of the proposed statements do you think would be most effective in advertising Bolda Cola? Why?

C. Is it possible that all four statements are based on the same survey data? Explain your reasoning.

D. In what other ways can you express the claims in the four proposed advertising statements? Explain.

E. If you were to survey 1,000 cola drinkers, what numbers of Bolda Cola and Cola Nola drinkers would you expect? Explain.

ACE Homework starts on page 10.

1.2 Targeting an Audience

Some middle and high school students earn money by delivering papers, mowing lawns, or baby-sitting. Students with money to spend are a target audience for some radio and television ads. Companies gather information about how much students watch television or listen to the radio. This information influences how they spend their advertising dollars.

As you work on this problem and the rest of the unit, you will see statements about ratio comparisons. In mathematics, it is acceptable to write ratios in different ways. Each way is useful.

Ways to Write a Ratio

3 to 2	3 : 2	$\frac{3}{2}$

It can be confusing to see a fraction representing a ratio. A ratio is usually, but not always, a *part-to-part* comparison. A fraction usually means a *part-to-whole* comparison. The context can help you decide whether a fraction represents a ratio.

Problem 1.2 Analyzing Comparison Statements

Students at Neilson Middle School are asked if they prefer watching television or listening to the radio. Of 150 students, 100 prefer television and 50 prefer radio.

A. How would you compare student preferences for radio or television?

B. Decide if each statement accurately reports results of the Neilson Middle School survey.

   1. At Neilson Middle School, $\frac{1}{3}$ of the students prefer radio to television.

   2. Students prefer television to radio by a ratio of 2 to 1.

   3. The ratio of students who prefer radio to television is 1 to 2.

   4. The number of students who prefer television is 50 more than the number of students who prefer radio.

   5. The number of students who prefer television is two times the number who prefer radio.

   6. 50% of the students prefer radio to television.

C. Compare statements in parts (4) and (5) above. Which is more informative? Explain.

D. Consider only the accurate statements in Question B.

   1. Which statement would best convince merchants to place ads on radio? Why?

   2. Which statement would best convince merchants to place ads on television? Why?

ACE Homework starts on page 10.

1.3 American Records

People are amazed and amused by records like the highest mountain, the longest fingernails, or the most spoons balanced on a face. What you have learned so far can help you make comparisons. In Problem 1.3, you will compare the largest living trees of different species.

Did You Know?

The champion white "Wye" oak tree near Wye Mills, Maryland, was about 460 years old when it fell during a thunderstorm in 2002. When the tree fell, thousands came by to gawk, shed tears, and pick up a leaf or a twig. Maryland officials carefully gathered and stored as much of the tree as they could until a suitable use could be found.

The challenge to find a white oak bigger than the Wye Mills tree launched the National Register of Big Trees. The search led to the discovery of a new national champion white oak in Virginia.

Go Online
PHSchool.com **For:** Information about big trees **Web Code:** ane-9031

You can describe the size of a tree by comparing it to other trees or familiar things.

Selected Champion Trees

Tree Type	Circumference (ft)	Height (ft)	Spread/Diameter (ft)
Giant Sequoia (Calif.)	83.2	275	107
Coast Redwood (Calif.)	79.2	321	80
Swamp Chestnut Oak (Tenn.)	23.0	105	216
Florida Crossopetalum (Fla.)	0.4	11	3
White Oak (Md.)	31.8	96	119

SOURCE: *Washington Post*

Problem **1.3** Writing Comparison Statements

A. Use the table on the previous page.

1. How many coast redwood spreads does it take to equal the spread of the white oak?

2. Kenning says that the spread of the white oak is greater than that of the coast redwood by a ratio of about 3 to 2. Is he correct? Explain.

3. Mary says the difference between the heights of the coast redwood and the giant sequoia is 46 feet. Is she correct? Explain.

4. How many giant sequoia spreads does it take to equal the spread of the swamp chestnut oak?

5. Jaime says the spread of the giant sequoia is less than 50% of the spread of the swamp chestnut oak. Is he correct?

6. Len says the circumference of the swamp chestnut oak is about three fourths the circumference of the white oak. Is he correct?

B. The tallest person in history, according to the *Guinness Book of World Records*, was Robert Wadlow. He was nearly 9 feet tall. Write two statements comparing Wadlow to the trees in the table. Use fractions, ratios, percents, or differences.

C. Average waist, height, and arm-span measurements for a small group of adult men are given.

Waist = 32 inches   Height = 72 inches   Arm Span = 73 inches

Write two statements comparing the data on these men to the trees in the table. Use fractions, ratios, percents, or differences.

D. When a problem requires comparison of counts or measurements, how do you decide whether to use differences, ratios, fractions, or percents?

ACE Homework starts on page 10.

Applications Connections Extensions

Applications

1. In a comparison taste test of two drinks, 780 students preferred Berry Blast. Only 220 students preferred Melon Splash. Complete each statement.

   a. There were ■ more people who preferred Berry Blast.

   b. In the taste test, ■% of the people preferred Berry Blast.

   c. People who preferred Berry Blast outnumbered those who preferred Melon Splash by a ratio of ■ to ■.

2. In a comparison taste test of new ice creams invented at Moo University, 750 freshmen preferred Cranberry Bog ice cream while 1,250 freshmen preferred Coconut Orange ice cream.

   Complete each statement.

   a. The fraction of freshmen who preferred Cranberry Bog is ■.

   b. The percent of freshmen who preferred Coconut Orange is ■%.

   c. Freshmen who preferred Coconut Orange outnumbered those who preferred Cranberry Bog by a ratio of ■ to ■.

3. A town considers whether to put in curbs along the streets. The ratio of people who support putting in curbs to those who oppose it is 2 to 5.

   a. What fraction of the people *oppose* putting in curbs?

   b. If 210 people in the town are surveyed, how many do you expect to *favor* putting in curbs?

   c. What percent of the people oppose putting in curbs?

Students at a middle school are asked to record how they spend their time from midnight on Friday to midnight on Sunday. Carlos records his data in the table below. Use the table for Exercises 4–7.

Weekend Activities

Activity	Number of Hours
Sleeping	18
Eating	2.5
Recreation	8
Talking on the Phone	2
Watching Television	6
Doing Chores or Homework	2
Other	9.5

4. How would you compare how Carlos spent his time on various activities over the weekend? Explain.

5. Decide if each statement is an accurate description of how Carlos spent his time that weekend.

   a. He spent one sixth of his time watching television.

   b. The ratio of hours spent watching television to hours spent doing chores or homework is 3 to 1.

   c. Recreation, talking on the phone, and watching television took about 33% of his time.

   d. Time spent doing chores or homework was only 20% of the time spent watching television.

   e. Sleeping, eating, and "other" activities took up 12 hours more than all other activities combined.

6. Estimate what the numbers of hours would be in *your* weekend activity table. Then write a ratio statement like statement (b) to fit your data.

7. Write other accurate statements comparing Carlos's use of weekend time for various activities. Use each concept at least once.

   a. ratio

   b. difference

   c. fraction

   d. percent

8. A class at Middlebury Middle School collected data on the kinds of movies students prefer. Complete each statement using the table.

Types of Movies Preferred by Middlebury Students

Type of Movie	Seventh-Graders	Eighth-Graders
Action	75	90
Comedy	105	150
Total	180	240

a. The ratio of seventh-graders who prefer comedies to eighth-graders who prefer comedies is ■ to ■.

b. The fraction of total students (both seventh- and eighth-graders) who prefer action movies is ■.

c. The fraction of seventh-graders who prefer action movies is ■.

d. The percent of total students who prefer comedies is ■.

e. The percent of eighth-graders who prefer action movies is ■.

f. Grade ■ has the greater percent of students who prefer action movies.

Homework Help Online
PHSchool.com
For: Help with Exercise 8
Web Code: ane-3108

9. Use the table.

Selected Champion Trees

Tree Type	Height (ft)	Spread (ft)
Florida Crossopetalum	11	3
White Oak	96	119

a. The height of the crossopetalum (kroh soh PET uh lum) is what fraction of the height of the white oak?

b. The height of the crossopetalum is what percent of the height of the white oak?

c. The spread of the crossopetalum is what fraction of the spread of the white oak?

d. The spread of the crossopetalum is what percent of the spread of the white oak?

10. In a survey, 100 students were asked if they prefer watching television or listening to the radio. The results show that 60 students prefer watching television while 40 prefer listening to the radio. Use each concept at least once to express student preferences.

a. ratio

b. percent

c. fraction

d. difference

Connections

11. A fruit bar is 5 inches long. The bar will be split into two pieces. For each situation, find the lengths of the two pieces.

   a. One piece is $\frac{3}{10}$ of the whole bar.

   b. One piece is 60% of the bar.

   c. One piece is 1 inch longer than the other.

12. Exercise 11 includes several numbers or quantities: 5 inches, 3, 10, 60%, and 1 inch. Determine whether each number or quantity refers to the whole, a part, or the difference between two parts.

The sketches below show two members of the Grump family. The figures are geometrically similar. Use the figures for Exercises 13–16.

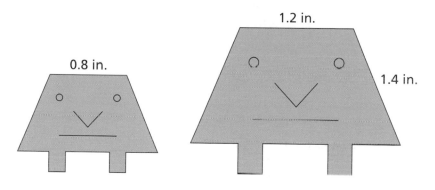

13. Write statements comparing the lengths of corresponding segments in the two Grump drawings. Use each concept at least once.

   a. ratio   **b.** fraction

   c. percent   **d.** scale factor

14. Write statements comparing the areas of the two Grump drawings. Use each concept at least once.

   a. ratio   **b.** fraction

   c. percent   **d.** scale factor

15. How long is the segment in the smaller Grump that corresponds to the 1.4-inch segment in the larger Grump?

16. **Multiple Choice** The mouth of the smaller Grump is 0.6 inches wide. How wide is the mouth of the larger Grump?

   A. 0.4 in.   **B.** 0.9 in.   **C.** 1 in.   **D.** 1.2 in.

The drawing below shows the Big Wheel spinner used in a game at the Waverly School Fun Night. It costs 20 cents to spin the wheel, and winners receive $1.00. The chart shows the data from 236 spins of the Big Wheel. Use the spinner and the chart for Exercises 17–21.

Win	Lose
46	190

17. The sectors of the spinner are identical in size. What is the measure in degrees of each central angle?

18. You play the game once. What is the theoretical probability that you win?

19. Do the results in the table agree with the probability statement you made in Exercise 18? Why or why not?

20. Write statements comparing the number of wins to the number of losses. Use each concept at least once.

    a. ratio   **b.** percent   **c.** difference

21. Which comparison from Exercise 20 is the best way to convey probability information about this game? Explain.

22. Copy the number line below. Add labels for 0.25, $\frac{6}{8}$, $1\frac{3}{4}$, and 1.3.

23. Write two unequal fractions with different denominators. Which fraction is greater? Explain.

24. Write a fraction and a decimal so that the fraction is greater than the decimal. Explain.

Copy each pair of numbers in Exercises 25–33. Insert <, >, or = to make a true statement.

25. $\frac{4}{5}$ ■ $\frac{11}{12}$ **26.** $\frac{14}{21}$ ■ $\frac{10}{15}$ **27.** $\frac{7}{9}$ ■ $\frac{3}{4}$

28. 2.5 ■ 0.259   **29.** 30.17 ■ 30.018   **30.** 0.006 ■ 0.0060

31. 0.45 ■ $\frac{9}{20}$ **32.** $1\frac{3}{4}$ ■ 1.5   **33.** $\frac{1}{4}$ ■ 1.3

Extensions

34. Rewrite this ad so that it will be more effective.

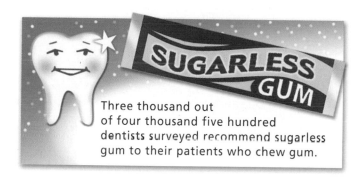

Three thousand out of four thousand five hundred dentists surveyed recommend sugarless gum to their patients who chew gum.

35. Use the table below.

Money Spent for Food

Where Food Is Eaten	1990	1998
Home	$303,900,000,000	$401,800,000,000
Away From Home	$168,800,000,000	$354,400,000,000

SOURCE: U.S. Census Bureau. Go to PHSchool.com for a data update. Web Code: ang-9041

a. Compare money spent on food eaten at home and food eaten away from home to the total money spent for food. Write statements for each year.

b. Explain how the statements you wrote in part (a) show the money spent for food away from home increasing or decreasing in relation to the total spent for food.

Use the table for Exercises 36–41.

Advertising Spending in the United States (millions)		
Placement	1990	2000
Newspapers	$32,281	$46,582
Magazines	$6,803	$11,096
Television	$29,073	$50,843
Radio	$8,726	$16,930
Yellow Pages	$8,926	$12,666
Internet	$0	$1,840
Direct Mail	$23,370	$41,601
Other	$20,411	$33,671
Total	$129,590	$215,229

SOURCE: U.S. Census Bureau. Go to **PHSchool.com** for a data update. Web code: ang–9041

36. Which placement has the greatest difference in advertising dollars between 1990 and 2000?

37. Find the percent of all advertising dollars spent on each placement in 1990.

38. Find the percent of all advertising dollars spent on each placement in 2000.

39. Use your results from Exercises 36–38. Write several sentences describing how advertising spending changed from 1990 to 2000.

40. Suppose you were thinking about investing in either a television station or a radio station. Which method of comparing advertising costs (differences or percents) makes television seem like the better investment? Which makes radio seem like the better investment?

41. Suppose you are a reporter writing an article about trends in advertising over time. Which method of comparison would you choose?

Mathematical Reflections 1

In this investigation, you explored several ways of comparing numbers. The problems were designed to help you understand and use different comparison strategies and recognize when each is most useful. The following questions will help you summarize what you have learned.

Think about your answers to these questions. Discuss your ideas with other students and your teacher. Then write a summary of your findings in your notebook.

1. Explain what you think each word means when it is used to make a comparison.

   a. ratio

   b. percent

   c. fraction

   d. difference

2. Give an example of a situation using each concept to compare two quantities.

   a. ratio

   b. percent

   c. fraction

   d. difference

Comparing Ratios, Percents, and Fractions

You used ratios, fractions, percents, and differences to compare quantities in Investigation 1. Now, you will develop strategies for choosing and using an appropriate comparison strategy. As you work through the problems, you will make sense of the statements in the *Did You Know?*

Did You Know?

- In 2001, 20.8% of all radio stations in the United States had country music as their primary format, while only 4.5% had a Top-40 format.

- For the first 60 miles of depth, the temperature of Earth increases 1°F for every 100 to 200 feet.

- In 2000, cancer accounted for about $\frac{1}{5}$ of all deaths in the United States.

- In 2001, silver compact cars and silver sports cars outsold black cars by a ratio of 5 to 3.

Go Online
PHSchool.com
For: Information about any of these topics
Web Code: ane-9031

Julia and Mariah attend summer camp. Everyone at the camp helps with the cooking and cleanup at meal times.

One morning, Julia and Mariah make orange juice for all the campers. They plan to make the juice by mixing water and frozen orange-juice concentrate. To find the mix that tastes best, they decide to test some mixes.

Mix A

2 cups concentrate   3 cups cold water

Mix B

5 cups concentrate   9 cups cold water

Mix C

1 cup concentrate   2 cups cold water

Mix D

3 cups concentrate   5 cups cold water

Problem 2.1 Developing Comparison Strategies

A. Which mix will make juice that is the most "orangey"? Explain.

B. Which mix will make juice that is the least "orangey"? Explain.

C. Which comparison statement is correct? Explain.

$\frac{5}{9}$ of Mix B is concentrate. $\frac{5}{14}$ of Mix B is concentrate.

D. Assume that each camper will get $\frac{1}{2}$ cup of juice.

    1. For each mix, how many batches are needed to make juice for 240 campers?

    2. For each mix, how much concentrate and how much water are needed to make juice for 240 campers?

E. For each mix, how much concentrate and how much water are needed to make 1 cup of juice?

ACE Homework starts on page 24.

The camp dining room has two kinds of tables. A large table seats ten people. A small table seats eight people. On pizza night, the students serving dinner put four pizzas on each large table and three pizzas on each small table.

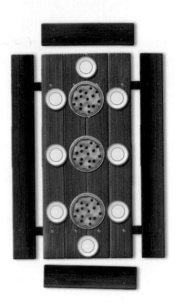

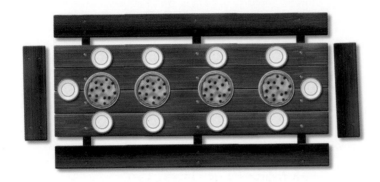

Problem 2.2 More Comparison Strategies

A. Suppose the pizzas are shared equally by everyone at the table. Does a person sitting at a small table get the same amount as a person sitting at a large table? Explain your reasoning.

B. Which table relates to $\frac{3}{8}$? What do the 3 and the 8 mean? Is $\frac{3}{8}$ a part-to-whole comparison or a part-to-part comparison?

C. Selena thinks she can decide at which table a person gets the most pizza. She uses the following reasoning:

   $10 - 4 = 6$ and $8 - 3 = 5$ so the large table is better.

   1. What does the 6 mean and what does the 5 mean in Selena's method of reasoning?

   2. Do you agree or disagree with Selena's method?

3. Suppose you put nine pizzas on the large table. What answer does Selena's method give? Does this answer make sense?

   4. What can you now say about Selena's method?

D. 1. The ratio of large tables to small tables in the dining room is 8 to 5. There are exactly enough seats for the 240 campers. How many tables of each kind are there?

    2. What fraction of the campers sit at small tables?

    3. What percent of the campers sit at large tables?

ACE Homework starts on page 24.

2.3 Finding Equivalent Ratios

It is often helpful, when forming ratios, to replace the actual numbers being compared with simpler numbers that have the same relationship to each other.

- People prefer Bolda Cola over Cola Nola by a ratio of 17,139 to 11,426, or 3 to 2.

- Students prefer television to radio by a ratio of 100 to 50, or 2 to 1.

- Monthly sales of *Reader's Digest* magazine exceed those of *National Geographic* by 11,044,694 to 6,602,650, or about 3 to 2.

Getting Ready for Problem 2.3

Suppose all classes at your grade level took the cola taste test. The result was 100 to 80 in favor of Bolda Cola.

- How do you scale down this ratio to make it easier to understand?

- What are some other ratios equivalent to this ratio in which the numbers are greater? Finding greater numbers is scaling *up* the ratio.

- How is scaling ratios like finding equivalent fractions for $\frac{100}{80}$? How is it different?

One of Ming's tasks at the county zoo's primate house is to mix food for the chimpanzees. The combination of high-fiber nuggets and high-protein nuggets changes as the chimps grow from babies to adults.

Ming has formulas for mixing high-fiber and high-protein nuggets for the chimps.

- Baby chimps: 2 cups high-fiber nuggets and 3 cups high-protein nuggets per serving
- Young adult chimps: 6 cups high-fiber nuggets and 4 cups high-protein nuggets per serving
- Older chimps: 4 cups high-fiber nuggets and 2 cups high-protein nuggets per serving

A. 1. What amounts of high-fiber and high-protein nuggets will Ming need when she has to feed 2 baby chimps? 3 baby chimps? 4 baby chimps?

Copy and complete the table below.

Dietary Needs of Baby Chimps

Number of Baby Chimps	1	2	3	4	5	10
Cups of High-Fiber Nuggets	▪	▪	▪	▪	▪	▪
Cups of High-Protein Nuggets	▪	▪	▪	▪	▪	▪

2. What patterns do you see in your table?

3. Ming puts 48 cups of high-protein nuggets into the baby chimp mix. How many cups of high-fiber nuggets does she put into the mix? Explain.

4. Ming has a total of 125 cups of mix for baby chimps. How many cups of high-fiber nuggets are in the mix? Explain.

B. 1. What is the ratio of high-fiber to high-protein nuggets for young adult chimps?

2. Scale this ratio up to show the ratio of high-fiber to high-protein nuggets that will feed 21 young adult chimps.

3. To feed 18 young adults, you need 108 cups of high-fiber nuggets and 72 cups of high-protein nuggets. Show how to scale down this ratio to feed 3 young adult chimps.

C. 1. Darla wants to compare the amount of high-fiber nuggets to the total amount of food mix for young adult chimps. She makes this claim:

"High-fiber nuggets are $\frac{3}{2}$ of the total."

Lamar says Darla is wrong. He makes this claim:

"High-fiber nuggets are $\frac{3}{5}$ of the total."

Who is correct? Explain.

2. What fraction of the total amount of food mix for older chimps is high-fiber nuggets?

3. Suppose the ratio of male chimps to female chimps in a zoo is 5 to 4. What fraction of the chimps are male?

4. Suppose $\frac{2}{3}$ of the chimps in a zoo are female. Find the ratio of female chimps to male chimps in that zoo.

ACE Homework starts on page 24.

Applications

As you work on the ACE exercises, try a variety of reasoning methods. Then think about conditions when each method seems most helpful.

1. Compare these four mixes for apple juice.

Mix W

| 5 cups concentrate | 8 cups cold water |

Mix X

| 3 cups concentrate | 6 cups cold water |

Mix Y

| 6 cups concentrate | 9 cups cold water |

Mix Z

| 3 cups concentrate | 5 cups cold water |

a. Which mix would make the most "appley" juice?

b. Suppose you make a single batch of each mix. What fraction of each batch is concentrate?

c. Rewrite your answers to part (b) as percents.

d. Suppose you make only 1 cup of Mix W. How much water and how much concentrate do you need?

2. Examine these statements about the apple juice mixes in Exercise 1. Decide whether each is accurate. Give reasons for your answers.

a. Mix Y has the most water, so it will taste least "appley."

b. Mix Z is the most "appley" because the difference between the concentrate and water is 2 cups. It is 3 cups for each of the others.

c. Mix Y is the most "appley" because it has only $1\frac{1}{2}$ cups of water for each cup of concentrate. The others have more water per cup.

d. Mix X and Mix Y taste the same because you just add 3 cups of concentrate and 3 cups of water to turn Mix X into Mix Y.

3. If possible, change each comparison of concentrate to water into a ratio. If not possible, explain why.

   a. The mix is 60% concentrate.

   b. The fraction of the mix that is water is $\frac{3}{5}$.

   c. The difference between the amount of concentrate and water is 4 cups.

4. At camp, Miriam uses a pottery wheel to make three bowls in 2 hours. Duane makes five bowls in 3 hours.

   a. Who makes bowls faster, Miriam or Duane?

   b. At the same pace, how long will it take Miriam to make a set of 12 bowls?

   c. At the same pace, how long will it take Duane to make a set of 12 bowls?

5. Guests at a pizza party are seated at 3 tables. The small table has 5 seats and 2 pizzas. The medium table has 7 seats and 3 pizzas. The large table has 12 seats and 5 pizzas. The pizzas at each table are shared equally. At which table does a guest get the most pizza?

6. For each business day, news reports tell the number of stocks that gained (went up in price) and the number that declined (went down in price). In each of the following pairs of reports, determine which is better news for investors.

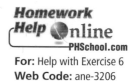

For: Help with Exercise 6
Web Code: ane-3206

   a. ⎡Gains outnumber declines by a ratio of 5 to 3.⎤   OR   ⎡Gains outnumber declines by a ratio of 7 to 5.⎤

   b. ⎡Gains outnumber declines by a ratio of 9 to 5.⎤   OR   ⎡Gains outnumber declines by a ratio of 6 to 3.⎤

   c. ⎡Declines outnumber gains by a ratio of 10 to 7.⎤   OR   ⎡Declines outnumber gains by a ratio of 6 to 4.⎤

7. Suppose a news story about the Super Bowl claims "Men outnumbered women in the stadium by a ratio of 9 to 5." Does this mean that there were 14 people in the stadium—9 men and 5 women? If not, what does the statement mean?

8. Multiple Choice Which of the following is a correct interpretation of the statement "Men outnumbered women by a ratio of 9 to 5?"

A. There were four more men than women.

B. The number of men was 1.8 times the number of women.

C. The number of men divided by the number of women was equal to the quotient of $5 \div 9$.

D. In the stadium, five out of nine fans were women.

Connections

9. If possible, change each comparison of red paint to white paint to a percent comparison. If it is not possible, explain why.

a. The fraction of a mix that is red paint is $\frac{1}{4}$.

b. The ratio of red to white paint in a different mix is 2 to 5.

10. If possible, change each comparison to a fraction comparison. If it is not possible, explain why.

a. The nut mix has 30% peanuts.

b. The ratio of almonds to other nuts in the mix is 1 to 7.

11. Find a value that makes each sentence correct.

a. $\frac{3}{15} = \frac{\blacksquare}{30}$ **b.** $\frac{1}{2} < \frac{\blacksquare}{20}$

c. $\frac{\blacksquare}{20} > \frac{3}{5}$ **d.** $\frac{9}{30} \leq \frac{\blacksquare}{15}$

e. $\frac{\blacksquare}{12} > \frac{3}{4}$ **f.** $\frac{9}{21} = \frac{12}{\blacksquare}$

12. Use the table to answer parts (a)–(e).

Participation in Walking for Exercise

	Ages 12–17	Ages 55–64
People Who Walk	3,781,000	8,694,000
Total in Group	23,241,000	22,662,000

SOURCE: U.S. Census Bureau. Go to **PHSchool.com** for a data update. Web Code: ang-9041

a. What percent of the 55–64 age group walk for exercise?

b. What percent of the 12–17 age group walk for exercise?

c. Write a ratio statement to compare the number of 12- to 17-year-olds who walk to the number of 55- to 64-year-olds who walk. Use approximate numbers to simplify the ratio.

d. Write a ratio statement to compare the percent of 12- to 17-year-olds who walk for exercise to the percent of 55- to 64-year-olds who walk for exercise.

e. Which data—actual numbers of walkers or percents—would you use in comparing the popularity of exercise walking among various groups? Explain.

13. The probability of getting a sum of 5 when you roll two number cubes is $\frac{4}{36}$. How many times should you expect to get a sum of 5 if you roll the cubes each number of times?

a. 9   **b.** 18   **c.** 27   **d.** 100   **e.** 450

14. For each diagram, write three statements comparing the areas of the shaded and unshaded regions. In one statement, use fraction ideas to express the comparison. In the second, use percent ideas. In the third, use ratio ideas.

a. 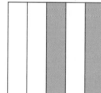   **b.**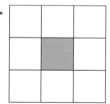

15. Multiple Choice Choose the value that makes $\frac{18}{30} = \frac{\blacksquare}{15}$ correct.

    F. 7   **G.** 8   **H.** 9   **J.** 10

16. Multiple Choice Choose the value that makes $\frac{\blacksquare}{15} \leq \frac{3}{5}$ correct.

    A. 9   **B.** 10   **C.** 11   **D.** 12

17. Find a value that makes each sentence correct. Explain your reasoning in each case.

For: Multiple-Choice Skills
Practice
Web Code: ana-3254

a. $\dfrac{3}{4} = \dfrac{\blacksquare}{12}$ **b.** $\dfrac{3}{4} < \dfrac{\blacksquare}{12}$ **c.** $\dfrac{3}{4} > \dfrac{\blacksquare}{12}$ **d.** $\dfrac{9}{12} = \dfrac{12}{\blacksquare}$

18. The sketches show floor plans for dorm rooms for two students and for one student.

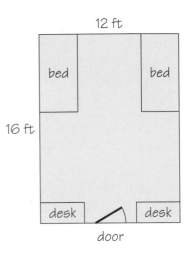
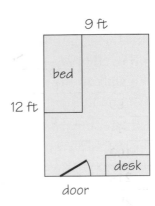

a. Are the floor plans similar rectangles? If so, what is the scale factor? If not, why not?

b. What is the ratio of floor areas of the two rooms (including space under the beds and desks)?

c. Which type of room gives more space per student?

19. Find values that make each sentence correct.

a. $\dfrac{6}{14} = \dfrac{\blacksquare}{21} = \dfrac{\blacksquare}{28}$ **b.** $\dfrac{\blacksquare}{27} = \dfrac{8}{36} = \dfrac{\blacksquare}{63}$

c. $\dfrac{\blacksquare}{20} = \dfrac{\blacksquare}{25} = \dfrac{6}{30}$ **d.** $\dfrac{\blacksquare}{8} = \dfrac{15}{\blacksquare} = \dfrac{24}{32}$

20. Suppose a news story reports, "90% of the people in the Super Bowl stadium were between the ages of 25 and 55." Alicia thinks this means only 100 people were in the stadium, and 90 of them were between 25 and 55 years of age. Do you agree with her? If not, what does the statement mean?

21. Suppose a news story reports, "A survey found that $\frac{4}{7}$ of all Americans watched the Super Bowl on television." Bishnu thinks this means the survey reached seven people and four of them watched the Super Bowl on television. Do you agree with him? If not, what does the statement mean?

Extensions

22. Mammals vary in the length of their pregnancies, or gestations. *Gestation* is the time from conception to birth. Use the table to answer the questions that follow.

Gestation Times and Life Spans of Selected Mammals		
Animal	**Gestation (days)**	**Life Span (years)**
Chipmunk	31	6
Cat	63	12
Fox	52	7
Lion	100	15
Black Bear	219	18
Gorilla	258	20
Moose	240	12
Giraffe	425	10
Elephant (African)	660	35

SOURCE: *The World Almanac and Book of Facts*

a. Plan a way to compare life span and gestation time for animals and use it with the data.

b. Which animal has the greatest ratio of life span to gestation time? Which has the least ratio?

c. Plot the data on a coordinate graph using (*gestation, life span*) as data points. Describe any interesting patterns that you see. Decide whether there is any relation between the two variables. Explain how you reached your conclusion.

d. What pattern would you expect to see in a graph if each statement were true?

   i. Longer gestation time implies longer life span.

   ii. Longer gestation time implies shorter life span.

23. The city of Spartanville runs two summer camps—the Green Center and the Blue Center. The table below shows recent attendance at the two camps.

	Green	Blue
Boys	125	70
Girls	75	30

In this exercise, you will show how several approaches can be used to answer the following question.

> Which center seems to offer a camping program that appeals best to girls?

a. What conclusion would you draw if you focused on the differences between the numbers of boy and girl campers from each center?

b. How could you use fractions to compare the appeal of the two centers' camping programs for boys and girls? What conclusion would you draw?

c. How could you use percents to compare the appeal of the two centers' camping programs for boys and girls? What conclusion would you draw?

d. How could you use ratios to compare the appeal of the two centers' camping programs for boys and girls? What conclusion would you draw?

24. Use the table below.

**Participation in Team Sports
at Springbrook Middle School**

Sport	Girls	Boys
Basketball	30	80
Football	10	60
Soccer	120	85
Total Surveyed	160	225

a. In which sport do boys most outnumber girls?

b. In which sport do girls most outnumber boys?

c. The participation in these team sports is about the same for students at Key Middle School.

  i. Suppose 250 boys at Key play sports. How many would you expect to play each of the three sports?

  ii. Suppose 240 girls at Key play sports. How many would you expect to play each of the three sports?

Extensions

Mathematical Reflections 2

In this investigation, you solved problems by comparing ratios, percents, and fractions. You also used ratio, percent, and fraction data to solve problems of larger or smaller scale. The following questions will help you summarize what you have learned.

Think about your answers to these questions. Discuss your ideas with other students and your teacher. Then write a summary of your findings in your notebook.

1. The director of a recreation center wants to compare the 10 boys to the 20 girls who attend its camping program.

   a. How would you make a comparison using fractions?

   b. How would you make a comparison using percents?

   c. How would you make a comparison using ratios?

   d. How is your percent comparison related to your ratio comparison?

   e. How is your fraction comparison related to your percent comparison?

2. a. Explain how you would scale up the ratio 10 boys to 14 girls to find equivalent ratios.

   b. Explain how you would scale down the ratio 10 boys to 14 girls to find equivalent ratios.

Investigation 3

Comparing and Scaling Rates

The following examples illustrate situations involving another strategy to compare numbers.

- My mom's car gets 45 miles per gallon on the expressway.
- We need two sandwiches for each person at the picnic.
- I earn $3.50 per hour baby-sitting for my neighbor.
- The mystery meat label says 355 Calories per 6-ounce serving.
- My brother's top running rate is 8.5 kilometers per hour.

Each of these statements compares two different quantities. For example, one compares miles to gallons of gas. A comparison of two quantities measured in different units is a **rate.** You have used rates in earlier problems. For example, you used rates in finding pizza per person.

Getting Ready for Problem 3.1

- What two quantities are being compared in the rate statements above?
- Which of the rate statements is different from the others?

3.1 Technology on Sale

Stores, catalogs, and Web sites often use rates in their ads. The ads sometimes give the cost for several items. You might see an offer like the one shown at the right.

Calculators for School

Fraction:	$120 for 20
Scientific:	$240 for 15
Graphing:	$800 for 10

The listed prices are for orders of 10, 15, or 20 calculators. But it's possible to figure the price for any number you want to purchase. One way to figure those prices is to build a *rate table*. A rate table is started below.

Price of Calculators for Schools

Number Purchased	1	2	3	4	5	10	15	20
Fraction Price	■	■	■	■	■	■	■	$120
Scientific Price	■	■	■	■	■	■	$240	■
Graphing Price	■	■	■	■	■	$800	■	■

Problem 3.1 Making and Using a Rate Table

Suppose you take orders over the phone for the calculator company. You should be quick with price quotes for orders of different sizes.

A. Build a rate table like the one above. Fill in prices for each type of calculator for orders of the sizes shown.

Use your rate table to answer Questions B–F.

B. How much does it cost to buy 53 fraction calculators? How much to buy 27 scientific calculators? How much to buy 9 graphing calculators?

C. How many fraction calculators can a school buy if it can spend $390? What if the school can spend only $84?

D. How many graphing calculators can a school buy if it can spend $2,500? What if the school can spend only $560?

E. What *arithmetic operation* (addition, subtraction, multiplication or division) do you use to find the cost per calculator?

F. Write an equation for each kind of calculator to show how to find the price for any number ordered.

ACE Homework starts on page 40.

3.2 Time, Rate, and Distance

Sascha cycled on a route with different kinds of conditions. Sometimes he went uphill, sometimes he went mostly downhill. Sometimes he was on flat ground. He stopped three times to record his time and distance:

- Stop 1: 5 miles in 20 minutes
- Stop 2: 8 miles in 24 minutes
- Stop 3: 15 miles in 40 minutes

Problem 3.2 Finding Rates

Show your work. Label any rate that you find with appropriate units.

A. Find Sascha's rate in miles per hour for each part of the route.

B. 1. On which part was Sascha cycling fastest? On which part was he cycling slowest?

   2. How do your calculations in Question A support your answers?

C. Suppose you can maintain a steady rate of 13 miles per hour on a bike. How long will it take you to travel the same distance Sascha traveled in 1 hour and 24 minutes?

D. Suppose you were racing Sascha. What steady rate would you have to maintain to tie him?

ACE Homework starts on page 40.

Did You Know?

The highest rate ever recorded on a pedal-powered bicycle was 166.944 miles per hour. Fred Rompelberg performed this amazing feat on October 3, 1995, at the Bonneville Salt Flats in Utah. He was able to reach this rate by following a vehicle. The vehicle acted as a windshield for him and his bicycle.

Go Online
PHSchool.com **For:** Information about speed records
Web Code: ane-9031

3.3 Comparing CD Prices

The ads below use rates to describe sale prices. To compare prices in sales such as these, it's often useful to find a unit rate. A **unit rate** is a rate in which one of the numbers being compared is 1 unit. The comparisons "45 miles per gallon," "$3.50 per hour," "8.5 kilometers per hour," and "two sandwiches for each person" are all unit rates. "Per gallon" means "for one gallon" and "per hour" means "for one hour."

Problem 3.3 Unit Rates and Equations

Use unit rates to compare the ad prices and to find the costs of various numbers of CDs at each store.

A. Which store has the lower price per CD?

B. For each store, write an equation (a rule) that you can use to calculate the cost c for any purchase of n compact discs.

C. Use the equations you just wrote for Question B. Write new equations to include 5% sales tax on any purchase.

D. Suppose a Web site sells CDs for $8.99 per disc. There is no tax, but there is a shipping charge of $5 for any order. Write an equation to give the cost c of any order for n discs from the Web site.

E. Use your equations from Question C or make a rate table to answer each question.

   1. How many discs do you have to order from the Web site to get a better deal than buying from Music City?

   2. How many discs do you have to order from the Web site to get a better deal than buying from CD World?

ACE Homework starts on page 40.

3.4 What Does Dividing Tell You?

In this problem, the questions will help you decide which way to divide when you are finding a unit rate. The questions will also help you with the meaning of the quotient after you divide.

Getting Ready for Problem 3.4

Dario has two options for buying boxes of pasta. At CornerMarket he can buy seven boxes of pasta for $6. At SuperFoodz he can buy six boxes of pasta for $5.

At CornerMarket, he divided 7 by 6 and got 1.16666667. He then divided 6 by 7 and got 0.85714286. He was confused. What do these numbers tell about the price of boxes of pasta at CornerMarket?

Decide which makes more sense to you. Use that division strategy to compare the two store prices. Which store offers the better deal?

Problem 3.4 Two Different Rates

Use division to find unit rates to solve the following questions. Label each unit rate.

A. SuperFoodz has oranges on sale at 10 for $2.

1. What is the cost per orange?

2. How many oranges can you buy for $1?

3. What division did you perform in each case? How did you decide what each division means?

4. Complete this rate table to show what you know.

Cost of Oranges at SuperFoodz						
Oranges	10	■	1	20	11	■
Cost	$2.00	$1.00	■	■	■	$2.60

B. Noralie used 22 gallons of gas to go 682 miles.

1. What are the two unit rates that she might compute?

2. Compute each unit rate and tell what it means.

3. Which seems more useful to you? Why?

C. It takes 100 maple trees to make 25 gallons of maple syrup.

   1. How many maple trees does it take for 1 gallon of syrup?

   2. How much syrup can you get from one maple tree?

D. A 5-minute shower requires about 18 gallons of water.

   1. How much water per minute does a shower take?

   2. How long does a shower last if you use only 1 gallon of water?

E. 1. At the CornerMarket grocery store, you can buy eight cans of tomatoes for $9. The cans are the same size as those at CannedStuff, which sells six cans for $5. Are the tomatoes at CornerMarket a better buy than the tomatoes at CannedStuff?

   2. What comparison strategies did you use to choose between CornerMarket and CannedStuff tomatoes? Why?

ACE **Homework starts on page 40.**

Applications

The problems that follow will give you practice in using rates (especially unit rates) in different situations. Be careful to use measurement units that match correctly in the rates you compute.

1. Maralah can drive her car 580 miles at a steady speed using 20 gallons of gasoline. Make a rate table showing the number of miles her car can be driven at this speed. Show 1, 2, 3, . . . , and 10 gallons of gas.

2. Joel can drive his car 450 miles at a steady speed using 15 gallons of gasoline. Make a rate table showing the number of miles his car can be driven at this speed. Show 1, 2, 3, . . . , and 10 gallons of gas.

3. Franky's Trail Mix Factory gives customers the following information. Use the pattern in the table to answer the questions.

Caloric Content of Franky's Trail Mix

Grams of Trail Mix	Calories
50	150
150	450
300	900
500	1,500

   a. Fiona eats 75 grams of trail mix. How many Calories does she eat?

   b. Rico eats trail mix containing 1,000 Calories. How many grams of trail mix does he eat?

   c. Write an equation that you can use to find the number of Calories in any number of grams of trail mix.

   d. Write an equation that you can use to find the number of grams of trail mix that will provide any given number of Calories.

For Exercises 4–8, you will explore relationships among time, rate, and distance.

4. When she drives to work, Louise travels 10 miles in about 15 minutes. Kareem travels 23 miles in about 30 minutes. Who has the faster average speed?

5. Rolanda and Mali ride bikes at a steady pace. Rolanda rides 8 miles in 32 minutes. Mali rides 2 miles in 10 minutes. Who rides faster?

6. Fasiz and Dale drive at the same speed along a road. Fasiz drives 8 kilometers in 24 minutes. How far does Dale drive in 6 minutes?

7. On a long dirt road leading to camp, buses travel only 6 miles in 10 minutes.

   a. At this speed, how long does it take the buses to travel 18 miles?

   b. At this speed, how far do the buses go in 15 minutes?

8. **Multiple Choice** Choose the fastest walker.

   A. Montel walks 3 miles in 1 hour.

   B. Jerry walks 6 miles in 2 hours.

   C. Phil walks 6 miles in 1.5 hours.

   D. Rosie walks 9 miles in 2 hours.

9. The dairy store says it takes 50 pounds of milk to make 5 pounds of cheddar cheese.

   a. Make a rate table showing the amount of milk needed to make 5, 10, 15, 20, . . . , and 50 pounds of cheddar cheese.

   b. Make a coordinate graph showing the relationship between pounds of milk and pounds of cheddar cheese. First, decide which variable should go on each axis.

   c. Write an equation relating pounds of milk m to pounds of cheddar cheese c.

   d. Explain one advantage of each method (the graph, the table, and the equation) to express the relationship between milk and cheddar cheese production.

10. A dairy manager says it takes 70 pounds of milk to make 10 pounds of cottage cheese.

   a. Make a rate table for the amount of milk needed to make 10, 20, . . . , and 100 pounds of cottage cheese.

   b. Make a graph showing the relationship between pounds of milk and pounds of cottage cheese. First, decide which variable should go on each axis.

   c. Write an equation relating pounds of milk m to pounds of cottage cheese c.

   d. Compare the graph in part (b) to the graph in Exercise 9. Explain how they are alike and how they are different. What is the cause of the differences between the two graphs?

11. A store sells videotapes at $3.00 for a set of two tapes. You have $20. You can split a set and buy just one tape for the same price per tape as the set.

   a. How many tapes can you buy?

   b. Suppose there is a 7% sales tax on the tapes. How many can you buy? Justify your solution.

For: Help with Exercise 11
Web Code: ane-3311

12. Study the data in these rate situations. Then write the key relationship in three ways:

   • in fraction form with a label for each part

   • as two different unit rates with a label for each rate

   a. Latanya's 15-mile commute to work each day takes an average of 40 minutes.

   b. In a 5-minute test, one computer printer produced 90 pages of output.

   c. An advertisement for a Caribbean cruise trip promises 168 hours of fun for only $1,344.

   d. A long-distance telephone call lasts 20 minutes and costs $4.50.

Connections

Rewrite each equation, replacing the variable with a number that makes a true statement.

13. $\frac{4}{9} \times n = 1\frac{1}{3}$

14. $n \times 2.25 = 90$

15. $n \div 15 = 120$

16. $180 \div n = 15$

17. Write two fractions with a product between 10 and 11.

18. Write two decimals with a product between 1 and 2.

A recent world-champion milk producer was a 4-year-old cow from Marathon, Wisconsin. The cow, Muranda Oscar Lucinda, produced a record 67,914 pounds of milk in one year! Use this information for Exercises 19–22.

19. Look back at your answers to Exercise 10. How much cottage cheese could be made from the amount of milk that Muranda Oscar Lucinda produced during her record year?

20. The average weight of a dairy cow is 1,500 pounds. How many dairy cows would be needed to equal the weight of the cottage cheese you found in Exercise 19?

21. One gallon of milk weighs about 8.7 pounds. Suppose a typical milk bucket holds about 3 gallons. About how many milk buckets would Muranda Oscar Lucinda's average daily production of milk fill?

22. One pound of milk fills about two glasses. About how many glasses of milk could you fill with Muranda Oscar Lucinda's average daily production of milk?

23. Some campers bike 10 miles for a nature study. Use this setting to write questions that can be answered by solving each equation. Find the answers, and explain what they tell about the bike ride.

    a. $10 \div 8 = \blacksquare$ **b.** $1.2 \times \blacksquare = 10$ **c.** $\blacksquare \div 2 = 5$

The table shows the mean times that students in one seventh-grade class spend on several activities during a weekend. The data are also displayed in the stacked bar graph below the table. Use both the table and the graph for Exercises 24 and 25.

Weekend Activities (hours)

Category	Boys	Girls	All Students
Sleeping	18.8	18.2	18.4
Eating	4.0	2.7	3.1
Recreation	7.8	6.9	7.2
Talking on the Phone	0.5	0.7	0.6
Watching TV	4.2	3.0	3.4
Doing Chores and Homework	3.6	5.8	5.1
Other	9.1	10.7	10.2

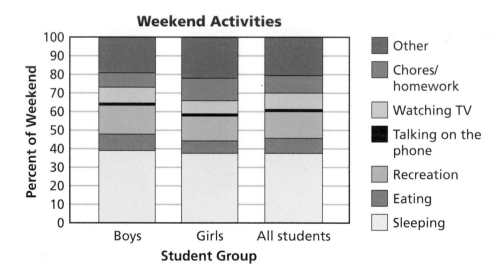

Weekend Activities

24. The stacked bar graph was made using the data from the table. Explain how it was constructed.

25. Suppose you are writing a report summarizing the class's data. You have space for either the table or the graph, but not both. What is one advantage of including the table? What is one advantage of including the stacked bar graph?

26. This table shows how to convert liters to quarts.

Liters	Quarts
1	1.06
4	4.24
5	5.30
9	9.54

    a. About how many liters are in 5.5 quarts?

    b. About how many quarts are in 5.5 liters?

    c. Write an equation for a rule that relates liters L to quarts Q.

Express each of the relationships in Exercises 27–31 as a unit rate. Label each unit rate with measurement units.

27. 12 cents for 20 beads

28. 8 cents for 10 nails

29. 405 miles on 15 gallons of gasoline

30. 3 cups of water for 2 cups of orange concentrate

31. $4 for 5 cans of soup

Go Online
PHSchool.com
For: Multiple-Choice Skills Practice
Web Code: ana-3354

32. The two clocks shown below are geometrically similar. One is a reduction of the other. Each outside edge of the larger clock is 2 centimeters long. Each outside edge of the smaller clock is 1.6 centimeters long.

    a. Write an equation relating the length L of any part of the large clock to the length S of the corresponding part of the small clock.

    b. Write an equation relating the area R of any part of the large clock to the area M of the corresponding part of the small clock.

    c. Write a decimal scale factor relating lengths in the large clock to lengths in the small clock. Explain how that scale factor is like a unit rate.

Extensions

33. Chemistry students analyzed the contents of rust. They found that it is made up of iron and oxygen. Tests on samples of rust gave these data.

Contents of Rust

Amount of Rust (g)	Amount of Iron (g)	Amount of Oxygen (g)
50	35.0	15.0
100	70.0	30.0
135	94.5	40.5
150	105.0	45.0

a. Suppose the students analyze 400 grams of rust. How much iron and how much oxygen should they find?

b. Is the ratio of iron to oxygen the same in each sample? If so, what is it? If not, explain.

c. Is the ratio of iron to total rust the same in each sample? If so, what is it? If not, explain.

34. A cider mill owner has pressed 240 liters of apple juice. He has many sizes of containers in which to pack the juice.

a. The owner wants to package all the juice in containers of the same size. Copy and complete this table to show the number of containers of each size needed to hold the juice.

Containers Needed by Volume

Volume of Container (liters)	10	4	2	1	$\frac{1}{2}$	$\frac{1}{4}$	$\frac{1}{10}$
Number of Containers Needed	■	■	■	■	■	■	■

b. Write an equation that relates the volume *v* of a container and the number *n* of containers needed to hold 240 liters of juice.

Mathematical Reflections 3

In this investigation, you learned to compare rates, to find unit rates, and to use rates to make tables and graphs and to write equations. The following questions will help you summarize what you have learned.

Think about your answers to these questions. Discuss your ideas with other students and your teacher. Then write a summary of your findings in your notebook.

The Picked Today fruit stand sells three green peppers for $1.50.

1. a. Describe the process for finding a unit rate for the peppers.

   b. Find two different unit rates to express the relationship between peppers and price. Explain what each unit rate tells.

   c. Fresh Veggie sells green peppers at five for $2.25. Compare Picked Today pepper prices with Fresh Veggie prices using two different kinds of unit rates.

   d. How do you decide whether the larger unit rate or the smaller unit rate is the better buy?

2. How would you construct a rate table for green pepper prices at the two vegetable stands? Explain what the entries in the table tell.

3. a. How would you write an equation to show the price for *n* peppers bought at Picked Today?

   b. Explain how the unit rate is used in writing the equation.

Making Sense of Proportions

In the following comparison problems, you have information about the relationship between quantities, but one or more specific values are unknown.

- **Calculators** Calculators are on sale at a price of $1,000 for 20. How many can be purchased for $1,250?

- **Similar Figures** The scale factor relating two similar figures is 2. One side of the larger figure is 10 centimeters long. How long is the corresponding side of the smaller figure?

- **Country Music** Country music is the primary format of 20% of American radio stations. There are about 10,600 radio stations in the United States. About how many stations focus on country music?

- **Doctors** Among American doctors, males outnumber females by a ratio of 15 to 4. If about 450,000 doctors are males, about how many are females?

Each of these problems can be solved in several ways. You will learn specific ways to set up ratios for problems like this and find missing values.

4.1 Setting Up and Solving Proportions

There are many ways to solve problems such as the ones on the previous page. One standard way is to create two ratios to represent the information in the problem. Then set these two ratios equal to each other to form a proportion. A **proportion** is an equation that states two ratios are equal.

For example, in the problem about doctors, you have enough information to write one ratio. Then write a proportion to find the missing quantity. There are four different ways to write a proportion representing the data in the problem.

Write the known ratio of male to female doctors. Complete the proportion with the ratio of actual numbers of doctors.

$$\frac{15 \text{ (male)}}{4 \text{ (female)}} = \frac{450{,}000 \text{ males}}{x \text{ females}}$$

Write a ratio of male to male data. Complete the proportion with female to female data.

$$\frac{15 \text{ (male)}}{450{,}000 \text{ males}} = \frac{4 \text{ (female)}}{x \text{ females}}$$

Write the known ratio of female to male doctors. Complete the proportion with the ratio of actual numbers of doctors.

$$\frac{4 \text{ (female)}}{15 \text{ (male)}} = \frac{x \text{ females}}{450{,}000 \text{ males}}$$

Write a different ratio of male to male data. Complete the proportion with female to female data.

$$\frac{450{,}000 \text{ males}}{15 \text{ (male)}} = \frac{x \text{ females}}{4 \text{ (female)}}$$

Using your knowledge of equivalent ratios, you can now find the number of female doctors from any one of these proportions.

Does any arrangement seem easier than the others?

Analyze the "Similar Figures" problem in the introduction.

The scale factor relating two similar figures is 2. One side of the larger figure is 10 centimeters long. How long is the corresponding side of the smaller figure?

- The scale factor means that the lengths of the sides of the larger figure are 2 times the lengths of the sides of the smaller. What is the ratio of the side lengths of the smaller figure to those of the larger figure?

- Write a proportion to represent the information in the problem.

- Solve your proportion to find the length of the corresponding side of the smaller figure.

Problem 4.1 **Setting Up and Solving Proportions**

A. Figure out whether each student's thinking about each line in the following problem is correct. Explain.

Dogs outnumber cats in an area by a ratio of 9 to 8. There are 180 dogs in the area. How many cats are there?

Adrianna's Work:

$$\frac{9 \text{ dogs}}{8 \text{ cats}} = \frac{180 \text{ dogs}}{x \text{ cats}}$$

$$\frac{9}{8} \times \frac{20}{20} = \frac{180}{160}$$

$$\frac{180}{160} = \frac{180}{x}$$

$$x = 160$$

1. Why did Adrianna multiply by $\frac{20}{20}$? How did she find what to multiply by?

2. What does this proportion tell you about the denominators? Why?

3. Is the answer correct? Explain.

Joey's Work:

$$\frac{8 \text{ cats}}{9 \text{ dogs}} = \frac{x \text{ cats}}{180 \text{ dogs}}$$

$$\frac{8}{9} = \frac{80}{90} = \frac{160}{180}$$

There are 160 cats.

4. What strategy did Joey use?

5. Why can he make this claim?

B. 1. Calculators are on sale at a price of $1,000 for 20. How many can be purchased for $1,250? Write and solve a proportion that represents the problem. Explain.

2. Country music is the primary format of 20% of American radio stations. There are about 10,600 radio stations in the United States. About how many stations focus on country music?

C. Use the reasoning you applied in Question B to solve these proportions for the variable *x*. Explain.

1. $\frac{8}{5} = \frac{32}{x}$ **2.** $\frac{7}{12} = \frac{x}{9}$ **3.** $\frac{25}{x} = \frac{5}{7}$ **4.** $\frac{x}{3} = \frac{8}{9}$

D. Use proportions to find the missing lengths in the following similar shapes.

1.

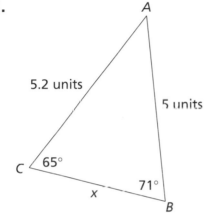

active math online

For: Scaling Figures Activity
Visit: PHSchool.com
Web Code: and-3401

2. Find the height of the tree.

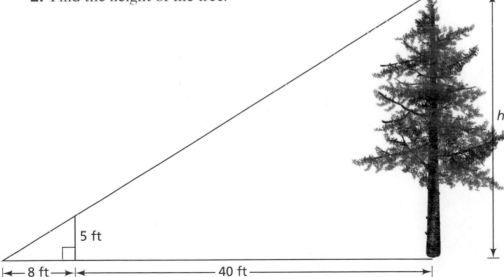

ACE Homework starts on page 55.

4.2 Everyday Use of Proportions

In our everyday lives, we often need to solve proportion problems. So do bakers, tailors, designers, and people in many other occupations.

You may have heard someone say, "A pint is a pound the world around." This saying suggests how to compare liquid measures with weight. It tells us that a pint of liquid weighs about a pound. If you drink a quart of milk a day, you might ask,

"About how much does a quart of liquid weigh?"

Problem 4.2 Applications of Proportions

A. Jogging 5 miles burns about 500 Calories. How many miles will Tanisha need to jog to burn off the 1,200-Calorie lunch she ate?

B. Tanisha jogs about 8 miles in 2 hours. How long will it take her to jog 12 miles?

C. Sam's grandmother says that "a stitch in time saves nine."

   1. What do you think Sam's grandmother means?

   2. Sam's grandmother takes 25 stitches in time. How many does she save?

D. Imani gives vitamins to her dogs. The recommended dosage is 2 teaspoons per day for adult dogs weighing 20 pounds. She needs to give vitamins to Bruiser, who weighs 75 pounds, and to Dust Ball, who weighs 7 pounds. What is the correct dosage for each dog?

E. The scale factor relating two similar figures is 1.8. One side of the larger figure is 12 centimeters. How long is the corresponding side of the smaller figure?

ACE **Homework starts on page 55.**

4.3 Developing Strategies for Solving Proportions

When mathematicians find the same kind of problem occurring often, they look for a systematic method, or algorithm, that can be applied in each case.

So far in this investigation, you have found ways to solve proportions in specific cases with nice numbers. Now you will develop general strategies that will guide you in solving proportions when the numbers are not so nicely related.

Problem 4.3 Developing Strategies for Solving Proportions

A. A jet takes 10 miles to descend 4,000 feet. How many miles does it take for the jet to descend 5,280 feet?

1. Set up two different proportions that can be solved to answer the question.

2. Solve one of your proportions by whatever method you choose. Check to see that your answer makes sense.

B. Jack works at a restaurant and eats one enchilada for lunch every day that he works. He figures that he ate 240 enchiladas last year. Three enchiladas have a total of 705 Calories. How many Calories did he take in last year from eating enchiladas?

1. Set up a proportion that can be solved to answer the question.

2. Solve your proportion. Check to see that your answer makes sense.

3. Describe each step in your solution strategy.

4. Can your strategy be used to solve any proportion? Explain.

5. How many Calories did he eat for lunch each working day?

C. In Pinecrest Middle School, there are 58 sixth-graders, 76 seventh-graders, and 38 eighth-graders. The school council is made up of 35 students who are chosen to represent all three grades fairly.

    1. Write fractions to represent the part of the school population that is in each grade.

    2. Use these fractions to write and solve proportions that will help you determine a fair number of students to represent each grade on the school council. Explain.

    3. How would the number of students from each grade change if the number of members of the school council were increased to 37? Explain your reasoning.

D. Ms. Spencer needs 150 graphing calculators for her math students. Her budget allows $5,000 for calculators. She needs to know if she can buy what she needs at the discount store where calculators are on sale at 8 for $284.

She writes the following statement:

$$\frac{8}{284} = \frac{150}{x} \quad \text{or} \quad \frac{8}{284} = 150 \div x$$

    1. Use fact-family relationships to rewrite the proportion so that it is easier to find x.

    2. Solve the proportion, recording and explaining each of your steps.

    3. Is your method a general method that can be used to solve any proportion? Explain.

ACE **Homework starts on page 55.**

Applications

1. Jared and Pedro walk 1 mile in about 15 minutes. They can keep up this pace for several hours.

   a. About how far do they walk in 90 minutes?

   b. About how far do they walk in 65 minutes?

2. Swimming $\frac{1}{4}$ of a mile uses about the same number of Calories as running 1 mile.

   a. Gilda ran a 26-mile marathon. About how far would her sister have to swim to use the same number of Calories Gilda used during the marathon?

   b. Juan swims 5 miles a day. About how many miles would he have to run to use the same number of Calories used during his swim?

3. After testing many samples, an electric company determined that approximately 2 of every 1,000 light bulbs on the market are defective. Americans buy more than 1 billion light bulbs every year. Estimate how many of these bulbs are defective.

4. The organizers of an environmental conference order buttons for the participants. They pay $18 for 12 dozen buttons. Write and solve proportions to answer each question. Assume that price is proportional to the size of the order.

   a. How much do 4 dozen buttons cost?

   b. How much do 50 dozen buttons cost?

   c. How many dozens can the organizers buy for $27?

   d. How many dozens can the organizers buy for $63?

Homework Help Online
PHSchool.com
For: Help with Exercise 4
Web Code: ane-3404

Investigation 4 Making Sense of Proportions **55**

5. Denzel makes 10 of his first 15 shots in a basketball free-throw contest. His success rate stays about the same for his next 100 free throws. Write and solve a proportion to answer each part. Round to the nearest whole number. Start each part with the original 10 of 15 free throws.

    a. About how many free throws does Denzel make in his next 60 attempts?

    b. About how many free throws does he make in his next 80 attempts?

    c. About how many attempts does Denzel take to make 30 free throws?

    d. About how many attempts does he take to make 45 free throws?

For Exercises 6–13, solve each equation.

6. $12.5 = 0.8x$ **7.** $\frac{x}{15} = \frac{20}{50}$ **8.** $\frac{x}{18} = 4.5$ **9.** $\frac{15.8}{x} = 0.7$

10. $\frac{5}{9} = \frac{12}{x}$ **11.** $245 = 0.25x$ **12.** $\frac{18}{x} = \frac{4.5}{1}$ **13.** $\frac{0.1}{48} = \frac{x}{960}$

Go Online
PHSchool.com
For: Multiple-Choice Skills Practice
Web Code: ana-3454

14. Multiple Choice Middletown sponsors a two-day conference for selected middle-school students to study government. There are three middle schools in Middletown.

Suppose 20 student delegates will attend the conference. Each school should be represented fairly in relation to its population. How many should be selected from each school?

North Middle School
618 students

Central Middle School
378 students

South Middle School
204 students

    A. North: 10 delegates, Central: 8 delegates, South: 2 delegates

    B. North: 11 delegates, Central: 7 delegates, South: 2 delegates

    C. North: 6 delegates, Central: 3 delegates, South: 2 delegates

    D. North: 10 delegates, Central: 6 delegates, South: 4 delegates

Connections

For Exercises 15–17, use ratios, percents, fractions, or rates.

15. **Multiple Choice** Which cereal is the best buy?

    F. a 14-ounce box for $1.98   **G.** a 36-ounce box for $2.59

    H. a 1-ounce box for $0.15   **J.** a 72-ounce box for $5.25

16. Which is the better average: 10 of 15 free throws, or 8 of 10 free throws?

17. Which is the better home-run rate: two home runs per 60 times at bat, or five home runs per 120 times at bat?

18. A jar contains 150 marked beans. Scott takes several samples from the jar and gets the results shown.

Bean Samples

Number of Beans	25	50	75	100	150	200	250
Number of Marked Beans	3	12	13	17	27	38	52
Percent of Marked Beans	12%	■	■	■	■	■	■

    a. Copy and complete the table.

    b. Graph the data using (*number of beans, marked beans*) as data points. Describe the pattern of data points in your graph. What does the pattern tell you about the relationship between the number of beans in a sample and the number of marked beans you can expect to find?

19. **Multiple Choice** Ayanna is making a circular spinner to be used at the school carnival. She wants the spinner to be divided so that 30% of the area is blue, 20% is red, 15% is green, and 35% is yellow. Choose the spinner that fits the description.

    A.

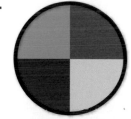

    B.

    C.

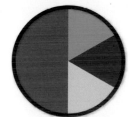

    D.

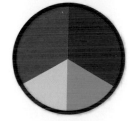

20. Hannah is making her own circular spinner. She makes the ratio of green to yellow 2 : 1, the ratio of red to yellow 3 : 1, and the ratio of blue to green 2 : 1. Make a sketch of her spinner.

21. a. Plot the points $(8, 6)$, $(8, 22)$, and $(24, 14)$ on grid paper. Connect them to form a triangle.

    b. Draw the triangle you get when you apply the rule $(0.5x, 0.5y)$ to the three points from part (a).

    c. How are lengths of corresponding sides in the triangles from parts (a) and (b) related?

    d. The area of the smaller triangle is what percent of the area of the larger triangle?

    e. The area of the larger triangle is what percent of the area of the smaller triangle?

22. The sketch shows two similar polygons.

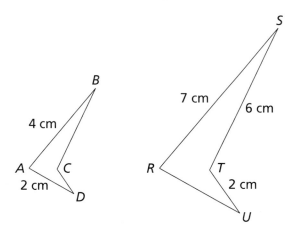

    a. What is the length of side BC?

    b. What is the length of side RU?

    c. What is the length of side CD?

23. To earn an Explorer Scout merit badge, Yoshi and Kai have the task of measuring the width of a river. Their report includes a diagram that shows their work.

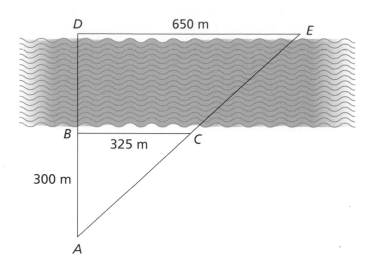

a. How do you think they came up with the lengths of the segments *AB*, *BC*, and *DE*?

b. How can they find the width of the river from segments *AB*, *BC*, and *DE*?

Extensions

24. Angela, a biologist, spends summers on an island in Alaska. For several summers she studied puffins. Two summers ago, Angela captured, tagged, and released 20 puffins. This past summer, she captured 50 puffins and found that 2 of them were tagged. Using Angela's findings, estimate the number of puffins on the island. Explain.

25. Rita wants to estimate the number of beans in a large jar. She takes out 100 beans and marks them. Then she returns them to the jar and mixes them with the unmarked beans. She then gathers some data by taking a sample of beans from the jar. Use her data to predict the number of beans in the jar.

> **Sample**
> Number of marked beans: 2
> Beans in sample: 30

26. The two histograms below display information about gallons of water used per person in 24 households in a week.

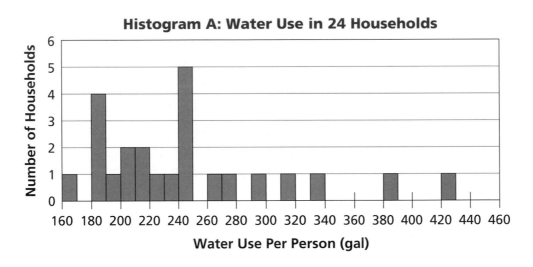

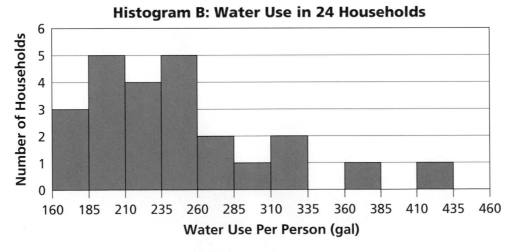

a. Compare the two histograms and explain how they differ.

b. Where do the data seem to clump in Histograms A and B?

27. The picture at the right is drawn on a centimeter grid.

 a. On a grid made of larger squares than those shown here, draw a figure similar to this figure. What is the scale factor between the original figure and your drawing?

 b. Draw another figure similar to this one, but use a grid made of smaller squares than those shown here. What is the scale factor between the original and your drawing?

 c. Compare the perimeters and areas of the original figure and its copies in each case (enlargement and reduction of the figure). Explain how these values relate to the scale factor in each case.

28. The people of the United States are represented in Congress, which is made up of the House of Representatives and the Senate.

 a. In the House of Representatives, the number of representatives from each state varies. From what you know about Congress, how is the number of representatives from each state determined?

 b. How is the number of senators from each state determined?

 c. Compare the two methods of determining representation in Congress. What are the advantages and disadvantages of these two forms of representation for states with large populations? How about for states with small populations?

Mathematical Reflections 4

In this investigation, you used ratios and proportions to solve a variety of problems. You found that most of those problems can be expressed in proportions such as $\frac{a}{b} = \frac{c}{x}$ or $\frac{a}{b} = \frac{x}{c}$. The next questions will help you summarize what you have learned.

Think about your answers to these questions. Discuss your ideas with other students and your teacher. Then write a summary of your findings in your notebook.

1. For each situation, write a problem that can be solved using a proportion. Then solve your problem.
   a. The fraction of girls in grade seven is $\frac{3}{5}$.
   b. Bolda Cola sells at 5 for $3.
   c. Sora rides her bike at a speed of 12 miles per hour.
   d. A triangle is similar to another one with a scale factor of 1.5.

2. Write four different proportions for the problem you created in part (c). Show that the answer to the problem is the same no matter which proportion you use.

3. What procedures do you use to solve proportions such as those you wrote in Question 2?

Unit Project

Paper Pool

The unit project is a mathematical investigation of a game called Paper Pool. For a pool table, use grid paper rectangles like the one shown at the right. Each outside corner is a pocket where a "ball" could "fall."

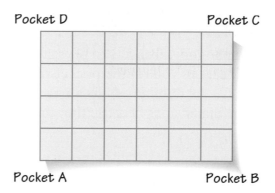

How to Play Paper Pool

- The ball always starts at Pocket A.
- To move the ball, "hit" it as if you were playing pool.
- The ball always moves on a 45° diagonal across the grid.
- When the ball hits a side of the table, it bounces off at a 45° angle and continues to move.
- If the ball moves to a corner, it falls into the pocket at that corner.

The dotted lines on the table at the right show the ball's path.

- The ball falls in Pocket D.
- There are five "hits," including the starting hit and the final hit.
- The dimensions of the table are 6 by 4 (always mention the horizontal length first).

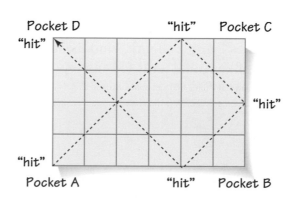

Part 1: Investigate Two Questions

Use the three Paper Pool labsheets to play the game. Try to find rules that tell you (1) the pocket where the ball will fall and (2) the number of hits along the way. Keep track of the dimensions because they may give you clues to a pattern.

Part 2: Write a Report

When you find some patterns and reach some conclusions, write a report that includes

- A list of the rules you found and an explanation of why you think they are correct
- Drawings of other grid paper tables that follow your rule
- Any tables, charts, or other tools that helped you find patterns
- Other patterns or ideas about Paper Pool

Extension Question

Can you predict the length of the ball's path on any size Paper Pool table? Each time the ball crosses a square, the length is 1 diagonal unit. Find the length of the ball's path in diagonal units for any set of dimensions.

For: Paper Pool Activity
Visit: PHSchool.com
Web Code: and-3000

Looking Back and Looking Ahead

The problems in this unit required you to compare measured quantities. You learned when it seems best to use subtraction, division, percents, rates, ratios, and proportions to make those comparisons. You developed a variety of strategies for writing and solving proportions. These strategies include writing equivalent ratios to scale a ratio up or down. You also learned to compute and reason with unit rates.

Go Online
PHSchool.com

For: Vocabulary Review Puzzle
Web Code: anj-3051

Use Your Understanding: Proportional Reasoning

Test your understanding of percents, rates, ratios, and proportions by solving the following problems.

1. There are 300 students in East Middle School. To plan transportation services for the new West Middle School, the school system surveyed East students. The survey asked whether students ride a bus to school or walk.

   - In Mr. Archer's homeroom, 20 students ride the bus and 15 students walk.

   - In Ms. Brown's homeroom, 14 students ride the bus and 9 students walk.

   - In Mr. Chavez's homeroom, 20 students ride the bus and the ratio of bus riders to walkers is 5 to 3.

   a. In what ways can you compare the number of students in Mr. Archer's homeroom who are bus riders to the number who are walkers? Which seems to be the best comparison statement?

   b. In what ways can you compare the numbers of bus riders and walkers in Ms. Brown's homeroom to those in Mr. Archer's homeroom? Again, which seems the best way to make the comparison?

   c. How many students in Mr. Chavez's homeroom walk to school?

d. Use the information from these three homerooms. About how many East Middle School students would you expect to walk to school? How many would you expect to ride a bus?

e. Suppose the new West Middle School will have 450 students and a ratio of bus riders to walkers that is about the same as that in East Middle School. About how many West students can be expected in each category?

2. The Purr & Woof Kennel buys food for animals that are boarded. The amounts of food eaten and the cost for food are shown below.

Cats:
$\frac{1}{3}$ pound per day

Small dogs:
$\frac{1}{2}$ pound per day

Large dogs:
$1\frac{1}{4}$ pounds per day

$5.98
Purr-fect CAT FOOD
10 Pounds

Bow-Chow Dog Food
50 Pounds
$24.50

a. Is cat food or dog food cheaper per pound?

b. Is it cheapest to feed a cat, a small dog, or a large dog?

c. On an average day, the kennel has 20 cats, 30 small dogs, and 20 large dogs. Which will last longer: a bag of cat food or a bag of dog food?

d. How many bags of dog food will be used in the month of January? How many bags of cat food will be used?

e. The owner finds a new store that sells Bow-Chow in 15 pound bags for $6.75 per bag. How much does that store charge for 50 pounds of Bow-Chow?

f. Which is a better buy on Bow-Chow: the original source or the new store?

Explain Your Reasoning

Answering comparison questions often requires knowledge of rates, ratios, percents, and proportional reasoning. Answer the following questions about your reasoning strategies. Use the preceding problems and other examples from this unit to illustrate your ideas.

3. How do you decide when to compare numbers using ratios, rates, or percents rather than by finding the difference of the two numbers?

4. Suppose you are given information that the ratio of two quantities is 3 to 5. How can you express that relationship in other written forms?

5. Suppose that the ratio of two quantities is 24 to 18.
   a. State five other equivalent ratios in the form "p to q."
   b. Use whole numbers to write an equivalent ratio that cannot be scaled down without using fractions or decimals.

6. What strategies can you use to solve proportions such as $\frac{5}{8} = \frac{12}{x}$ and $\frac{5}{8} = \frac{x}{24}$?

7. How does proportional reasoning enter into the solution of each problem?
   a. You want to prepare enough of a recipe to serve a large crowd.
   b. You want to use the scale of a map to find the actual distance between two points in a park from their locations on the map.
   c. You want to find which package of raisins is the better value.
   d. You want to use a design drawn on a coordinate grid to make several larger copies and several smaller copies of that design.

Look Ahead

Proportional reasoning is an important way to compare measured quantities. It includes comparing numerical information by ratios, rates, and percents. It is used in geometry to enlarge and reduce figures while retaining their shapes. You will apply proportional reasoning in future *Connected Mathematics* units such as *Filling and Wrapping*, *Moving Straight Ahead*, and *What Do You Expect?*

English/Spanish Glossary

P

proportion An equation stating that two ratios are equal. For example:

$$\frac{\text{hours spent on homework}}{\text{hours spent in school}} = \frac{2}{7}$$

Note that this does not necessarily imply that hours spent on homework = 2 or that hours spent in school = 7. During a week, 10 hours may have been spent on homework while 35 hours were spent in school. The proportion is still true because $\frac{10}{35} = \frac{2}{7}$.

proporción Una ecuación que indica que dos razones son iguales. Por ejemplo:

$$\frac{\text{horas dedicadas a la tarea}}{\text{horas en la escuela}} = \frac{2}{7}$$

Fíjate que esto no implica necesariamente que las horas dedicadas a la tarea = 2, ó que las horas en la escuela = 7. Durante una semana, puedes haber pasado 10 horas haciendo tarea y 35 horas en la escuela. La proporción sigue siendo verdadera porque $\frac{10}{35} = \frac{2}{7}$.

R

rate A comparison of quantities measured in two different units is called a rate. A rate can be thought of as a direct comparison of two sets (20 cookies for 5 children) or as an average amount (4 cookies per child). A rate such as 5.5 miles per hour can be written as $\frac{5.5 \text{ miles}}{1 \text{ hour}}$, or 5.5 miles : 1 hour.

tasa Una comparación de cantidades medidas en dos unidades diferentes se llama tasa. Una tasa se puede interpretar como una comparación directa entre dos grupos (20 galletas para 5 niños) o como una cantidad promedio (4 galletas por niño). Una tasa como 5.5 millas por hora se puede escribir como $\frac{5.5 \text{ millas}}{1 \text{ hora}}$, o como 5.5 millas a 1 hora.

rate table You can use a rate to find and organize equivalent rates in a rate table. For example, you can use the rate "five limes for $1.00" to make this rate table.

tabla de tasas Puedes usar una tasa para hallar y organizar tasas equivalentes en una tabla de tasas. Por ejemplo, puedes usar la tasa "cinco limas por $1.00" para hacer esta tabla de tasas, en la cual se indica el número de limas y el costo de las limas.

Cost of Limes

Number of Limes	1	2	3	4	5	10	15	20
Cost of Limes	$0.20	$0.40	$0.60	$0.80	$1.00	$2.00	$3.00	$4.00

ratio A ratio is a number, often expressed as a fraction, used to make comparisons between two quantities. Ratios may also be expressed as equivalent decimals or percents, or given in the form $a : b$. Here are some examples of uses of ratios:

- The ratio of females to males on the swim team is 2 to 3, or $\frac{2 \text{ females}}{3 \text{ males}}$.
- The train travels at a speed of 80 miles per hour, or $\frac{80 \text{ miles}}{1 \text{ hour}}$.
- If a small figure is enlarged by a scale factor of 2, the new figure will have an area four times its original size. The ratio of the small figure's area to the large figure's area will be $\frac{1}{4}$. The ratio of the large figure's area to the small figure's area will be $\frac{4}{1}$, or 4.
- In the example above, the ratio of the length of a side of the small figure to the length of the corresponding side of the large figure is $\frac{1}{2}$. The ratio of the length of a side of the large figure to the length of the corresponding side of the small figure is $\frac{2}{1}$, or 2.

razón Una razón es un número, a menudo expresado como fracción, que se usa para hacer comparaciones entre dos cantidades. Las razones también se pueden expresar como decimales equivalentes o porcentajes, o darse de la forma $a : b$. Estos son algunos ejemplos del uso de razones:

- La razón entre mujeres y hombres en el equipo de natación es 2 a 3, es decir, $\frac{2 \text{ mujeres}}{3 \text{ hombres}}$.
- El tren viaja a una velocidad de 80 millas por hora, o sea, $\frac{80 \text{ millas}}{1 \text{ hora}}$.
- Si se amplía una figura pequeña por un factor de escala 2, la nueva figura tendrá un área cuatro veces mayor que su tamaño original. La razón entre el área de la figura pequeña y el área de la figura grande será $\frac{1}{4}$. La razón entre el área de la figura grande y el área de la figura pequeña será $\frac{4}{1}$, o sea, 4.
- En el ejemplo anterior, la razón entre la longitud de un lado de la figura pequeña y la longitud del lado correspondiente de la figura grande es $\frac{1}{2}$. La razón entre la longitud de un lado de la figura grande y la longitud del lado correspondiente de la figura pequeña es $\frac{2}{1}$, o sea, 2.

S

scale, scaling The scale is the number used to multiply both parts of a ratio to produce an equal, but possibly more informative, ratio. A ratio can be scaled to produce a number of equivalent ratios. For example, multiplying the rate of 4.5 gallons per hour by a scale of 2 yields the rate of 9 gallons per 2 hours. Scales are also used on maps to give the relationship between a measurement on the map to the actual physical measurement.

escala, aplicar una escala La escala es el número que se usa para multiplicar las dos partes de una razón para producir una razón igual, pero posiblemente más informativa. Se puede aplicar una escala a una razón para producir un número de razones equivalentes. Por ejemplo, al multiplicar la razón de 4.5 galones por hora por una escala de 2, se obtiene una razón de 9 galones por 2 horas. Las escalas también se usan en los mapas para indicar la relación que existe entre una distancia en el mapa y una distancia real.

U

unit rate A unit rate is a rate in which the second number (usually written as the denominator) is 1, or 1 of a quantity. For example, 1.9 children per family, 32 miles per gallon, and $\frac{3 \text{ flavors of ice cream}}{1 \text{ banana split}}$ are unit rates. Unit rates are often found by scaling other rates.

tasa unitaria Una tasa unitaria es una tasa en la que el segundo número (normalmente escrito como el denominador) es 1 ó 1 de una cantidad. Por ejemplo, 1.9 niños por familia, 32 millas por galón, y $\frac{3 \text{ sabores de helado}}{1 \text{ banana split}}$ son tasas unitarias. Las tasas unitarias se calculan a menudo aplicando escalas a otras tasas.

Index

Index

Acknowledgments

Team Credits

The people who made up the **Connected Mathematics2** team—representing editorial, editorial services, design services, and production services—are listed below. Bold type denotes core team members.

Leora Adler, Judith Buice, Kerry Cashman, Patrick Culleton, Sheila DeFazio, Richard Heater, **Barbara Hollingdale, Jayne Holman,** Karen Holtzman, **Etta Jacobs,** Christine Lee, Carolyn Lock, Catherine Maglio, **Dotti Marshall,** Rich McMahon, Eve Melnechuk, Kristin Mingrone, Terri Mitchell, **Marsha Novak,** Irene Rubin, Donna Russo, Robin Samper, Siri Schwartzman, **Nancy Smith,** Emily Soltanoff, **Mark Tricca,** Paula Vergith, Roberta Warshaw, Helen Young

Additional Credits

Diana Bonfilio, Mairead Reddin, Michael Torocsik, nSight, Inc.

Illustration

Michelle Barbera: 41, 53, 67

Technical Illustration

WestWords, Inc.

Cover Design

tom white.images

Photos

2 t, Richard Hutchings/PhotoEdit; **2 m,** Alden Pellett/The Image Works; **2 b,** Kevin Schafer/Corbis; **3,** M. Barrett/Robertstock.com; **5,** Stockbyte; **8,** AP Photo/Easton Star Democrat, Chris Polk; **9,** Grant Heilman Photography; **11,** PhotoDisc/Getty Images, Inc.; **16,** Russ Lappa; **18,** Ron Kimball/Ron Kimball Stock; **20,** Richard Haynes; **23,** Martin Harvey/Peter Arnold, Inc.; **25,** Richard Hutchings/PhotoEdit; **29,** Art Wolfe/Getty Images, Inc.; **30,** Ariel Skelley/Corbis; **33,** Larry Kolvoord/The Image Works; **35,** Sam Kleinman/Corbis; **36,** Digital Vision/Getty Images, Inc.; **39,** Alden Pellett/The Image Works; **41,** Peter Johansky/Index Stock Imagery; **43,** Lester Lefkowitz/Getty Images, Inc.; **46,** Kevin Radford/SuperStock; **48,** Zoran Milich/Masterfile; **52,** Renee Stockdale/Animals Animals/Earth Scenes; **55,** Felix Stensson/Alamy; **59,** Kevin Schafer/Corbis; **61,** Sandy Schaeffer/Mai/Mai/Time Life Pictures/Getty Images, Inc.; **61 frame,** Karen Beard/Getty Images, Inc.; **64,** Richard Haynes